TH_I

At Hanging Rock, Australia - 2003

Edition 1

First published in September 2020

ISBN-13 : 9798684106279

Author's Website :   www.jackballentyne.co.uk

Instagram :   @jackballentynebooks

THE GAP LIFE

In the writing and publishing of this collection of stories, thanks are owed to many people, from those with starring roles in the events to those who convinced me to write the book and who offered their suggestions, reviews and corrections. However, as absolutely none of them want to be publicy associated with the book for fear of eternal ridicule, I won't include any names - you know who you are - and I'll simply say thanks to all ...."Without whom.....".

Disclaimer: All the events depicted in this book as based on real-life occurrences. Whilst the places are accurately identified and most of which can be visited today, the names of almost all the players have been changed and none may be construed as referring to a particular real-life person - so they don't sue me.

Three names, however, were not changed.

Percy, St. Christopher, and a particular bastard called Vincent.

THE GAP LIFE

Contents

INTRODUCTION

Ever been shot at? Chased by bandits in the freezing heights of the Andes? Or mistaken for a Soldier of fortune in South Africa, or tried to rob a bank with a water pistol? Sailed across the Atlantic in a leaking old sailboat, or had a chance encounter with the Pope? How about whitewater rafting the Zambezi...without a raft?

Episodes such as these, together with many more adventures and travels are what my life has been all about. They've been the driving force, and looking back, I can tell you, it's been a helluva ride!

Now, speaking of life, some people believe that we only have one, and when it's over, it's over. That's it.

Personally, even though I do believe in re-incarnation, my position is that there's no guarantee that you'll be coming back as another person, like a Nepalese Sherpa, but that your next episode could well be in a completely different form of life - a squid perhaps?

So, knowing that your time on earth is limited, "Live life to the full!" they say. "Live everyday like it's your last!" Nice idea, and easier said than done, especially if you are a normal person with a job, a mortgage, family, limited finances and even more importantly, limited time.

Modern life for the majority has become a bit of a treadmill. Over a lifetime, the amount of time spent on "adventure" versus time spent on the "treadmill" certainly favours being a hamster. Worse still, and sooner than you'd like, youth gives way to middle age, and things start aching, creaking and wrinkling.

Ah, but wait! Retirement is to be looked forward to – it's your time, free from obligations or the commitment of employment. If you do actually manage to reach the official retirement age, most average folks will spend a good-sized chunk of their hard-earned free time and money at the doctors or the dentists, and not white-water rafting the Zambezi.

My point here is that most of us spend our most able and adventurous years getting a job, toiling away at work, with twenty-or-so days a year of holidays for momentary respite. It's the norm.

If you are wondering where I'm going with all this, it's basically to introduce myself as someone who is a bit different and, whether by choice or chance, has approached life from a somewhat different philosophy. And I still do!

At an early age I seemed to develop a taste for craziness and travelling. Back then in the eighties, life seemed to be a lot more innocent and fun. Adventure seemed to be much more readily available.

I never had much money, and I really can't be certain what actually kicked things off, but to date I have been fortunate enough to have visited over seventy countries, some for short stays, some for several months, and some for several years.

I've almost become that squid sooner than expected on more than one occasion. Some countries I left happily, vowing to return, some countries I left quickly to avoid the prospect of a jail cell, but every country has left me with many memories and stories to tell.

When I started travelling, things were considerably different compared to today. Take trains for example.

Trains used to be romantic, exciting, classy. European train stations were just so exotic! The smells, the sounds, the people, the incomprehensible signs in a foreign language, no English translations.

There was first class, with eccentric and stylish travellers. There were second class compartments, each with a sliding door, in which six complete strangers were obliged to sit together for hours on end. Exchanges were inevitable. Folks didn't sit and purposely isolate themselves from the rest of the world with headphones and smartphones, sticking up a social middle finger at any kind of interaction. People spoke to one another. It was exhilarating.

And air travel? Economy class back then was like today's business class without the flat-bed seats. There were no security checks at airports, no on-line check-in. Remember the paper tickets? In-flight smoking was allowed in the back rows, and more dramatically, there was no in-flight entertainment.

You sat, you slept, you ate, you spoke with your fellow passengers, got names and phone numbers, swapped stories, you drank together, sometimes for hours on a long-haul flight.

Aircrew were glamorous, always smiling, always attractive, always attentive. You always wondered how they could look so good at 5am after a ten-hour flight when you looked like a hobo and had a mouth like the bottom of a birdcage.

Times have changed and sadly things have gone in a very sterile, un-adventurous way. Modern travel has turned people into sheep. Technology, supposedly a boon to mankind, in my books is not doing us as a race, too much of a favour. It's speeding everything up and isolating people.

In my mind, those are the two biggest social impacts technology is bringing to the masses. I don't have a smartphone even today. Just a simple Nokia for making calls and sending texts. It's fine. I can drop it on the floor without a worry that the screen will crack.

I could fill a book just with just the transport aspects of my travelling experiences…trains, boats, from small sailing boats through cargo ships and ferries to sailing across the Atlantic, buses, cars, planes and even animals. But, at the end of the day, transport is simply a means to get you from A to B. This book is not a travel book, painting descriptive pictures of distant lands, but more a collection of stories about my adventures in some of these B's I have visited.

Today, there are a lot of B's out there where you can still enjoy the feeling of being away from it all. Like going to another world in another time without the effects of humanity. Mass tourism and cheap package holidays don't go to these places – you need to seek them out and make and effort. Such places are what fuelled my travel bug way back in the 80's and which still remains with me today.

I'll take a moment here to mention that I am terrified of flying, which is strange for a bloke who loves travelling. The funny thing is, small planes and helicopters, old planes even, don't worry me in the slightest. Like the time I flew in a Tiger Moth biplane, open cockpit, upside down round a racetrack at a motor-sport event, hanging off the seatbelt. It was awesome!

What do terrify me are the big, modern sardine-can, wide-bodied jets. Three hundred tons of packed-in passengers and high-octane fuel. If anything goes wrong, that's it - a massive ball of flame! Without exaggeration, I don't sleep for several days before going on a modern long-haul flight.

Anyway, enough of that. Back to why we're here, hoping you still are! Home for me has always been some part or other of England. I had a stab at trying to become a Frenchman in France for a few years, and an even shorter stab at trying to become Spanish in Spain. An indication of the success of these stabs is given by the fact that today, home remains England.

Apart form my first job out of Uni, I have never held a full-time job for more than a few months. I've started several of my own companies, I've binned several of my own companies, I've built a bunch of properties, I've been through one marriage and veered off a second one at the last moment. My fixed abodes are invariably short-term and most definitely un-fixed, so no mortgage, no dependents, and no children - at least that that I am aware of.

No ties, no boss and no long-term commitments. It's interesting how many people I meet on my travels who tell me how envious they are of my situation. Is it that the grass really is greener....?

I have around sixty photo albums full of memories and stories that are simply awesome.   Photo albums? Sorry, but I still make prints of my best photographs and don't store millions of digital images in a cloud never to be looked at again.

As fate or destiny has taken me on this roller-coaster ride over the last forty years, there is no doubt that St. Christopher has consistently been looking out for me. He'll have winced many times and most definitely had to intervene more than once to avoid the birth of another squid. I must remember to put a good bottle of malt for him in the box when I finally do go!

Just before we kick things off then, I'll mention now that I decided to write this book mainly due enthusiastic persuasion from family, friends and many folks I have met in one bar or another. Apparently, I can tell an amusing tale and I do have a lot of tales to tell. I seem to have a gift for creating an audience in whichever watering hole I find myself. Maybe it's because I often wind up inviting everyone to a drink?

Now, telling a tale over a pint in the pub is one thing, especially when the audience has had a few themselves and are generally more easily entertained. But writing it down, such that an anonymous reader (that's you), in whatever mood or circumstances you find yourself at the time, gets the same quality of entertainment is an entirely different proposal. Still, I have the stories, so I'll have a go.

Finally, why "The Gap Life"? Many students after finishing university, eager to continue milking their parents (or the state's) till for extended fun and debauchery, take a Gap year off to travel round the world or go to some whacky place for a year or so before jumping onto the treadmill of modern life.

In my case, I have adopted this same Gap philosophy to pretty much every one of the last thirty years, only without milking anyone else's till. I work, I save, then disappear off for a few weeks, months, or years, then come back to Blighty, bruised, battered, bronzed and always skint. Then I'll do it all again.

My hope is that you might crack a smile or two reading this book, but more importantly make you realize that not only is there a great big wonderful, natural world out there, but more importantly you only have one shot to see it before it all changes for the worse. Seven nights all-inclusive in Punta Cana once a year just doesn't do it. Remember, the younger you are, the more you can do, so don't leave it too late!

All the stories in this book are one-hundred percent true and have not been exaggerated at all. I have, however, changed the characters' names in most to avoid offence or lawsuits.

On my travels, I've met thousands of colourful characters, good and bad, male and female, and have always been accompanied by more than the occasional beer, good music and the overpowering beauty and majesty of Mother Nature.

Embrace it if you can.

JB

PART I - THE EARLY YEARS

THE SOWING OF THE SEEDS

With a collection of stories like this, the first problem I had was to decide how and where to start.

They say that the early part of your life shapes you for the future. As my Dad was in the military and my adolescence was consequently a series of house moves, different schools and different friends, this is where I suspect the seeds of vagrancy, independency and abnormality were sown.

So, we'll start in North London, mid-Seventies.

Isn't it marvellous?   There I was, just into puberty, several months bumbling around like a drooling lap dog after Tina Crawford, completely smitten as one is at fifteen years old. Strong emotions those were. Two months of sweating, sleepless nights and saving up my pennies to build up the courage to ask her out. If she came within twenty yards of me at school, or, God forbid, an unintentional encounter in the corridor, a scarlet flush and total bowel release threatened. Shy, reserved type, I was.

So, what happens? The very day that I learn through the adolescent grapevine (remember, no social media then) that the untouchable Tina had decided to become touchable and that intimacy with yours truly was on the cards at the next house party, I get home from school and hear that Dad has quit the military, taken the pension and decided to go and live by the sea. On the south coast. As in a long bloody way away from London and Tina. I was devastated.

In a matter of weeks, we move from London to Devon, lock, stock and barrel. There's me, a spotty adolescent in love and am suddenly plucked out of emotional paradise and shuttled across the country through strangely named counties like Dorset to the English outback, Devon. Where the hell is Devon? The emotional scarring started early.

As was to be expected, those early days in Devon were remembered as being spent in total dejection. Tina was out of the window and most likely offering her touchability to some other dork, the thought of which drove me to the depths of despair.

I was condemned to the social wilderness of a new home, living with my parents in Devon for God's sake! In those days there was no Internet, Skype or anything of the sort. I had to plead to use the telephone, as it was apparently expensive to call London.

The phone was in the sitting room, so no chance of a private conversation. No cordless in those days. I remember it well, a big cream thing with a rotating dialer. I did manage to call Tina one evening, but her Mum said she was out with her boyfriend. I didn't call again.

Home was now a small, rented cottage in a sea-side retirement town full of grey hairs and Zimmer-frames. Of course, as with all moves, came yet another new school. I think this was now my sixth experience of being the "New-Boy".

I must admit though, to my surprise, things moved quickly in the right direction, socially speaking.

At sixteen, I entered the lower sixth, which meant no more school uniform and access to the common-room, the student-only lounge no teachers ever entered, and the freedom to play poker whenever we could. Remember again, no mobiles, no internet, no online porn, no Facebook or Instagram. Just social interaction, boys, girls, constant intrigue, flirting, gossip and banter. Glorious. The sun was starting to come out in Devon!

Of course, the new boy tag soon wore off and I made new friends quickly, finding myself in an inseparable group of like-minded imbeciles. It was these times and individuals which undoubtedly shaped my youth and on whom I well and truly place all blame for the loose-screw element in me.

Box, Spud, Spikey and Grub (yes, we all had one-word pseudonyms) were my best mates. Sounds like Gardeners World, but the Devon youth of those days were nutters, especially as my mates' Dads were all well-to-do local businessmen. This had certain advantages like being able to borrow nice cars, vans, houses for parties, and even boats.

A great deal of the craziness, the fun, the happy-go-luckiness that seems to have kept me company for a good part of my life germinated in these early days. We didn't intentionally live every day like it was our last, but on many occasions it certainly should have been. St. Christopher was obviously doing some early recruiting and probably budgeting for the future.

I'll give you a few examples.

Those were the days before massed and cheap package tourism allowed youngsters to mass-rave in particularly cool parts of Europe with more money than sense and everything laid on for them in English. In those simple times, Devon' s coast – both north and south - was the place for vacations and water sports. In the late seventies, surfing, and especially windsurfing was the big thing.

The small town we lived in on Devon's south coast was famous for its palatial Victorian seaside hotels and as a retirement community for well-to-do old folks – and believe me, there were some seriously old folks. They would shuffle along the promenade aided by walking sticks, Zimmer frames, wheelchairs, or just sit in the deck chairs and gaze out at whatever there was to watch on the water.

The Devon sea varied in character, changing from a flat, sparkling deep-blue, nothing to envy the Algarve for, to a grey-green, freezing choppiness. On the bad days, fierce mud-brown waves pounded the shingle beach. Admittedly, the times it was like the Algarve weren't the most frequent.

The beach was shingle. Round stones, pretty to look at, advantageous compared to sand in that stones don't get in your ice-cream or in "yer bits" and cause a rash, but a bugger to walk on in bare feet. The beach was probably on average about thirty to fifty yards wide from promenade to wet stuff, steeply sloping down as you approached the water's edge.

This meant that picking your way down to the water was the easy bit, as gravity sped you on your way. However, hauling yourself out of the water when you're knackered from fighting the waves, the current, the cold and the undertow and clambering back up the beach with the shingle crucifying the soles of your bare feet was hellishly painful.

Strange how crossing the pebbles in bare feet always requires one to have one's arms outstretched above the horizontal and wave them around like windsocks. Go to any pebble beach in summer and you'll see what I mean.

Anyway, on the few sunny days there were in a year in southern England, a pleasant enough time could be had at the beach.

And the beach was our domain.

I had one of the first windsurfers. Enormous thing it was, the size of a barn door, almost five meters long and weighing about fifteen kilos dry. I'll come back to that.

It had a fibre-glass outer shell painted red and white, filled with expanded foam inside. Great big, six square-meter sail, and a wooden centreboard which you could pull up or push down with your foot or using a rope loop. Very early technology.

My board was second-hand, had more patches than Grannie's quilt and suffered a new crack in the outer shell just about every time I used it. Still, it was my board and all I could afford.

As the beach was stony and steeply sloping, the waves pummelled you mercilessly into the shingle on launching and on returning. That meant my board acquired more cracks every time I used it, meaning it soaked up water, meaning it weighed about fifteen kilos when you went in…and about one hundred and fifty kilos when you came out!

An hour's windsurfing also meant that you were completely knackered from the exertions, so many was the time you could see this figure – me - staggering out of the pounding grey waves trying to stay on his feet, hauling this deadweight up the forty-five degree beach, leg muscles screaming in agony, hands blue with cold, soles of the feet being crucified by the pebbles, looking and feeling like he'd just been washed up from New Zealand.

For those of you that have never tried it, the difficult part about starting to windsurf is getting up on the board and getting the sail out of the water without falling off. Once standing up on the board, you then need to get the sail up out of the water to fill with wind. When you do manage to get up on the board, you need to make sure you get it facing the right direction, haul the sail out of the water, get some wind in it …then it's off-you-go!

Ha ha! Not so! Long before any "off-you-going" starts, you'll have fallen in the freezing water about a thousand times, be close to hypothermia, will have had to clamber back on the board two thousand times (that's because it would take a couple of re-mounting attempts for every falling off), turn the board into the right position versus the wind, drag the sail round, all the time being tossed around by the waves coming at you from all sides. Exhausting. Truly.

We all count calories today, and I certainly don't remember ever hearing the word "calorie" outside of

Mr. Johnson's excruciatingly boring physics lessons back in the day. I've been to the gym quite a few times in later life and know what it takes to burn five hundred calories. I reckon an hour's windsurfing in those conditions must have consumed thousands of calories. There wasn't an ounce of fat on me.

Anyway, with persistence and lots of energy spent, I soon became pretty good on the old windsurfer and could launch with relative ease. I'd swagger down the beach with the board under one arm, launch it into the breakers and hop on and sail away without hardly getting wet. The "off-you-going" was a matter of routine. And yes, it provided good free entertainment for all the old biddies sitting on the esplanade waiting expectantly for you to take the early bath.

Nutter #1 – Box

One particularly fine day, Box announced to all that he had shelled out a hundred and fifty quid on a "fun board", and would I teach him how to windsurf? That was a lot of money in those days.

I agreed, on the condition that I could have a go on his board at some point. For those who don't know what a Fun-board is, it was shorter, lighter and lost the centreboard to three small fins on the back like a real surfboard. A Fun-board in those days was new technology, a racing machine...like comparing a black-and-white tube TV (my board) with flat screen LED (fun-board). The Fun-board, however, was a damn sight more difficult to master and this was Box's first board. A little ambitious.

So, the wind's up, the sun's out, the promenade's full of elderly folk eagerly expecting something to watch, deck chair sales are booming, and we rendezvous on the beach.

I was the expert and I started Box off with the basics. He wobbles down the pebbles into the breakers with the board under one arm and wades in up to his chest, using the now floating board to maintain his balance. He works the board round to the right position, all the time being knocked back and forth by the incoming waves, and starts to attempt to clamber up onto it, which is what you really shouldn't don't do on Funboard, but what the hell? I stood at the water's edge yelling instructions, insults, encouragement, and generally laughing my socks off. As soon as Box managed to stand up on the wildly rocking board for a second or two and tried to pull the sail out of the water, he would promptly fall over backwards into the sea. And had to try again. And again. And again.

The wind was blowing onshore, so that every time he wiped out, which was in fact every time he managed to stand up on the board, he was automatically blown back to the relative safety of a beach-pummelling.

Anyway, this went on for about half an hour and, hat's off to Box, as just ten minutes of that would be the equivalent of a full body work out in today's gym. I was getting bored by now sitting on the beach, the shingle was making my ass numb and cold, and the entertainment value of watching Box repeatedly getting up and falling in soon lost its appeal

I decied to go for a drink, so shouted to him "I'm off — I'll wait for you in the Anchor!" That was our local bar up on the promenade, where I was soon joined by a couple of other blokes.

Around three hours later, after he was released from hospital, Box finally turned up and told us what had happened.

"I was doing ok, managing to stand-up on the board and actually getting the sail up out of the water, when all of a sudden, this gust came, filled the sail with the force of a bleedin' tow-truck and I shot forward like a bloody bullet. I held on for dear life, leant back and there I was, flyin'! Man, I was going like shit off a shovel, bouncing off the wave tops, almost leaving the water. I was leaning so far back I even managed a couple of head dips!"

He went on, as we listened whilst nursing our pints.

"The board was slapping over the waves and it felt like a hundred miles an hour. Bleedin' awesome! I must have been going for about five minutes, heading straight for France with no way to turn around. The wind was unbelievable. Suddenly, a gust came from behind so strong I couldn't hold it and the sail catapulted me forward over the front of the board. Must've gone ten feet in the air. Luckily, the board stopped dead – it could've killed me at that speed".

He continued. "It was only when I came up to surface that I realized it was now blowing a friggin' hurricane offshore, I was about a mile out to sea and completely buggered. My arms were totally knackered, and I was friggin' freezing. No chance of getting the sail back out of the water. I was in the shit, big time!".

Now, un-beknown to Box in his out-to-sea predicament, things had been happening on the promenade. People were watching and a crowd had gathered, sensing drama! The same kind of collective excitement a herd of Antelope might feel when a nearby predator is scented.

A bloke was in trouble, in rough seas, a long way out. Somebody called the police, somebody else called the coast guard, and somehow a reporter from the local newspaper headed down to the front with camera in hand. The Zimmer-frames were taking up station forming a line of stationary steel support along the promenade like an impromptu crowd barrier.

Meanwhile, Box, inspired by either quick-wittedness or sheer survival instinct, had managed to tie his board to a lobster pot marker buoy, and was kneeling on the board, waving to the massing crowd on the distant promenade as hypothermia started to set in. The local lifeboat was launched, as were a couple of local fishing boats.

In addition to the small-boat armada, as luck would have it, a Royal Navy Air-Sea Rescue helicopter was on exercises in the area and soon clattered into view over the nearby cliffs, heading towards the stranded Box, who by this time was slowly turning blue on the lobster pot.

There were now probably two hundred onlookers on the promenade, brandishing binoculars, monocles, cameras, walking sticks, anything that could be brandished. This was big news for the town.

The helicopter starts to hover above Box, flattening the sea in a fifty-yard circle around him. The winchman signals down to him to grab hold of the bottom of the rope ladder which was being lowered down, and to climb up a few rungs and hang on. They would then fly him to the shore.

Box, hardly able to move for the cold, gesticulated upwards that he wanted to take his expensive new Fun-board as well, which was still moored to the lobster pot. The helicopter was having none of it. The fleet of fishing boats were approaching and would probably retrieve it and sell it back to Box later.

So down comes the ladder, the lower rungs whipping around in the wind. A blue-bodied, red-faced Box, now suffering from severe fatigue, hypothermia, and acute embarrassment, manages to grab hold. The winchman, seeing Box on the lower rung, signals to the pilot and the chopper slowly rises and swivels round to head towards the beach. It gathered speed to some fifty miles an hour, with Box dangling thirty feet below just above the waves.

As the chopper gets over the beach, it slowed while descending, and the winchman gesticulated down to Box to jump off the ladder onto the beach. Box took the cue. However, acutely aware of the hundreds of onlookers, and needing to restore some of the lost face with a touch of derring-do for the benefit of the spectators, he leapt a few moments too soon and with a little less care than was warranted.

The bottom rung went up between his legs, one leg got caught and he promptly turned upside down, hanging now by his entwined right leg. The chopper pilot, seeing Box let go and assuming his cargo had been safely deposited on dry shingle, promptly pressed helicopter pedal to helicopter metal and decided to put on a show for the crowd by zooming off down the beach at great speed. Unbeknown to him, he still had an inverted Box dangling below, who's bonce was now bouncing over the pebbles.

Fortunately for the now half-unconscious Box, the helicopter then started to go up and at the same time head back out to sea. At some fifty feet in the air, and the same number of feet out to sea, Box's foot freed itself from the ladder, and to the clicks of hundreds of cameras and pensioners gasps, Box plummeted head first back into the English Channel like the rewind of a Trident missile launch.

Even though Baywatch didn't exist in those times, the local equivalent rushed to his aid, dragging him ashore to a waiting ambulance.

After a few hours in A&E and intravenous hot tea, he was released with a few cuts and bruises, mild concussion, one leg slightly longer than the other and improving hypothermia. The embarrassment didn't go so easily.

So about four hours after I had left him, Box shuffles into The Anchor.

"Shit, Box, you were a long time! How'd it go? We could hear a helicopter out there...did you see it?"

The following Saturday in the local rag Classifieds. "For sale, Fun board, Hardly Used, One careful Owner"

Nutters #2 and #3 – Spikey and Spud

Spikey had well-off parents, which enabled him to have what seemed to be an unlimited supply of booze, cars, surfboards, and even a speedboat. The girls obviously came with that. Not bad when you're seventeen. On any given Saturday, if not on our way to Croyde Bay to surf, we'd be water-skiing around Dawlish Warren near Exmouth.

On one such occasion, Spud came with us on his first water-skiing outing. It was all very exciting for him and, for different reasons, for Spikey and me also.

Now, I need to give you a picture of the River Exe estuary. It was very wide, probably a mile or two across, quite a strong tide, not very deep and peppered with all sorts of floating things. Boats mainly and thousands of mooring buoys, ranging from the size of a football for small dinghies, to the size of huge oil drums for trawlers, catamarans and small ocean-going freighters. Also, there was an abundance of coloured cardinals. These were metal structures sticking out of the water, a couple of meters tall, and painted different colours indicating the location of the many hidden sandbanks when the tide was in. These sandbanks could be treacherous for boats as they were often only covered by a few inches under the water at high tide.

So, all in all, an obstacle course of buoys, boats and hidden sandbanks scattered over an open stretch of water which was generally pretty busy with boats of all shapes and sizes coming and going, especially on the weekends in summer.

Challenging for a fast speedboat. Very challenging for a fast speedboat with a water-skier in tow. Total mayhem for a fast speed boat, a psychotic driver and accomplice, and a novice water-skier at their mercy.

As it was Spud's debut at water-skiing, it was decided that he should go first, at least to see if he could manage to get up out of the water.

With Spikey at the wheel – sorry, helm - and me acting as ski-master, engine burbling, Spud was all set in the water, fifty yards behind the boat, skis in the correct position jutting out of the water in front of him and just his head and shoulders visible.

"Hit it!" I ordered Spikey, who, bereft of any formal nautical training and understanding, and in the sadistic knowledge of having a complete novice water-skier out back, figured that you need to give it everything the boat's got to get the inept water-skier out of the water. The outboard roared with a hundred and fifty horses of life, the back of the boat dug in and we shot forward.

Now, the slack between boat and Spud got used up pretty bloody quickly. We could see Spud's face with a determined look on it, no doubt with all intent to show what a natural he was. Having skied a lot myself, I knew Spud was completely unaware of the amount of force that was about to be applied to his arms in a split second.

And it was. Half a ton of speed boat now going at twenty knots was transmitted down the rope which snapped taught and Spud did a good impression of a small explosion in the water, disappearing in a mass of white froth. Spikey and I grinned.

Then, lo and behold Spud's head appears, then his upper body, until he is completely out of the water. His arms were stretched out in front like a bloke lost in the dark, his arse sticking out the back with his body bent at ninety degrees but, nonetheless up on the skis. Once the foam had cleared, his face switched from sheer terror to a big grin - he could see that we could see him. Grinning like a Cheshire cat, he was. He was shouting something, but there was no way we could hear him.

Now, one of our games, when it was just Spikey and me, was to ski around the estuary seeking out the smaller buoys like a slalom. The idea was to go over them, letting them pass between your legs. I gesticulated to Spud who was fifty yards back and was now not grinning at all, as the initial euphoria of getting up had been replaced by sheer terror of the implications of falling over at the speed at which he was travelling. Couple that with a total lack of any kind of control over his destiny and he wasn't in the best of positions.

In the back of the boat, I enacted the positions of jumping a buoy as best I could, trying to stay upright, jumping up and down, opening my legs and pointing downwards between them. Spud hung on out back, probably wondering why the hell I was gesticulating towards my nuts.

Spikey sped the boat past by a small buoy and I pointed it out to Spud, who had about three milli-seconds to nod in acknowledgement and apparent understanding. All credit due, he opened his legs at the last second and successfully managed to pass over the buoy, a huge look of triumph on his face.

The fact I hadn't collapsed in laughter told Spikey that things weren't going as they should, and that he needed to up the ante. He promptly set about hunting another buoy at maximum speed. I know he was thinking the same as me - this wasn't supposed to happen, and Spud wasn't playing fair and giving us the entertainment that we had been expecting.

At this point Spikey spots another buoy, this time about the size of a space hopper. For those who don't remember the Space Hopper, they were big, inflatable rubber spheres about 3 feet across.

At the speed at which we were travelling, it was about three seconds away including a hard-right turn. Spikey went for it and the boat immediately heeled in and changed course ninety degrees towards the Hopper. But Spud didn't. Well, not immediately anyway.

Anyone who has water-skied knows what happens when the boat changes course very suddenly. The rope goes slack for a few moments before again taking up the tension, only at a different angle. With Spud now still on the original tack, and the boat now going off to his right, the rope slackens, and Spud slows down and starts to sink.

To counteract this effect, he desperately lifted his arms above his head to take up the slack in the rope. That was fine, but immediately the boat off to his right then reached the fifty yards rope length away and took up the slack in a very violent manner.

With the tow-bar held high above and back from his head, the rope suddenly returned to its former tension only this time at an angle and Spud gets jerked violently sideways and then proceeds on a totally out-of-control acceleration on a much wider curve going twice the speed of the boat.

We're now talking arms-being-pulled-out-of-sockets forces here, but Spud stays up. His face, however, is now a picture of terror as he has copped what's about to happen, has seen the hopper zooming towards him and knew he had no way out. A bit like a pig that is just about to get its throat slit - wild, primaeval rolling of the eyes and the knowledge that this is THE moment! One supposes Spud could have simply dropped the towbar, but we didn't do such things then.

The boat shot past the Hopper in a perfect trajectory to ensure that Spud was on a direct collision course at maximum speed. He's seen it coming at him, knows it won't fit between his legs so decides to lift one leg up and get one ski out of the water, just managing to pass over the orange globe without getting his knackers ripped off.

He then managed to continue for another hundred yards on one leg evidently not wanting to risk getting the airborne ski back in the water and certain obliteration.

Now it was starting to get entertaining!

Eventually Spud managed to get the airborne ski down and was on two stable feet again. By this time, he was yelling at us for all he was worth, and I hope the family in the nearby dinghy couldn't hear him because I'm sure it wasn't nice.

We certainly couldn't hear him, not that we were interested, as both Spikey and I could hardly see for the tears of laughter. This was more like it!

Still, we weren't satisfied. "Jammy bastard, he's still up" I yelled to Spikey, who nodded in agreement. More testing targets were needed.

Spud's arms by this time were probably a good six inches longer than when he'd started out, but still he hung on. Spikey swung the boat, still at full throttle around a large, rusty old freighter, just in time to pass an equally rusty barrel buoy about the size of a small car.

We shot past it at about thirty knots, giving Spud no chance to avoid the impossible. With a few seconds to contemplate death, the barrel rushing towards him, his eyes like a couple of golf balls, he bent his knees, tried to leap and in doing so, sucked his feet out of the rubber ski shoes. Now airborne, ski-less and still hanging on to the tow rope, the skis smash into the barrel while Spud flew over the top, arms out front like Superman.

Spikey dropped the power, Spud pirouetted in the air before plunging into the Exe at thirty miles per hour, his shorts disappearing up his bum at the same speed. I thought my gut was going to burst with laughter.

We burbled back and recovered the broken skis and fished Spud out. Once aboard, and after he'd pulled his swimming costume out of his colon, he then launched a thousand expletives at us, but we were still laughing too much to listen. To this day I am convinced his arms were longer than his legs at that moment, and Spud was a pretty lanky lad.

As Spud started to calm down and see the funny side of things, a serious speed boat thundered by, doing maybe thirty knots. A Fletcher. Twenty-five feet long, gleaming blue and white, with a bloody great Evinrude outboard on the back. White leather interior, good sound system. Expensive bit of kit. The bloke driving it was probably our age, another bloke sprawled in the back, drinking beer and doing his best to look Mr. Cool. Sunning themselves on the boat's foredeck were the two obligatory bikini babes, who probably came as an optional extra with the boat. They sped by, cocky as hell and laughing at the carnage in our boat. Especially the young skipper.

Now that's the same skipper who should have been watching out for sand bank cardinals and who wasn't.

His lovely Fletcher hit the hidden sandbank and went from thirty knots to no knots in a milli-second, which as you can imagine produces some interesting results. The two babes shot off the bow at, yep, thirty knots and landed – sorry, watered - somewhere up-estuary, flailing limbs and bikini bums skipping off the surface twice before disappearing into the brine.

The Skipper behind the wheel basically ate it (the wheel that is!), Mr. Cool in the back did a good impression of Spud's shorts, using the skipper's arse up which to disappear head first, and - most impressively of all - the top of the Evinrude engine blew off into the sky in a huge cloud of blue smoke like a submarine missile launch.

Having just calmed down from Spud's flying lessons, we three were now once again experiencing that hysterical laughter that is impossible to describe and stays with you for the rest of your life.

After a short time, we burbled over to them and mopped up, towing the stricken vessel back to the jetty.

To finish off a perfectly splendid day, Spikey got one of the girls' phone numbers.

How does the song go?   "Some guys have all the luck".

And last, but by no means least, we have Grub.

Nutter #4 – Grub

Grub was a biker. Hell's Angel's stereotype. A big, heavy-set bloke who looked about fifty even though he was our age. Thick, long, bushy and generally dirty red hair, an unkempt beard, a rotund face, and skin that at any given time was caked in a sheen of Havoline motor oil.

When his clothes got a bit grubby, and hence the nickname, he'd just put another layer on top. Add to this the obligatory leather jacket and a belt made up of three Triumph Trident drive chains welded together and that was Grub.

Visually, Grub would cause old ladies to hurl themselves over the nearest hedge if they saw him approaching, but he was a gentle giant and well educated to boot. I have a hundred tales to tell about Grub, but just one particular event will sum him up.

It was a steaming August day, height of the tourist season, and the pebble beach was packed. The sea was a beautiful calm Algarve blue - yes, one of those days – the sail boats were floating, airbeds and blow-up dinghies bobbing close to the shore with the Dads freezing their balls off playing with their kids at the water's edge. The entire town was out on the Promenade, Zimmer-frames gleaming, deck chairs galore, bunting on the shops and lamp posts, a real British summer seaside picture-postcard scene.

Me, Box and Spikey were chilling out on the pebbles in our beach kit of the time, surrounding a pile of six packs, when lo and behold, Grub staggered out of The Marine Bar like something out of Micheal Jackson's Thriller video, only significantly more intoxicated.

He spotted us, yelled something totally incoherent, and bounded over the road and promenade towards us. The flocks of old ladies on the Prom, Zzimmer frames, deck-chairs and all, parted like the Red Sea, only a bit slower, to let the lumbering Grub leap off the prom down the almost six-foot drop onto the pebbles.

He landed three feet from an unsuspecting family of day-trippers, showering them and anyone else in a ten-foot radius with pebbles. I'm sure if you look at a seismograph of southern England on that day, the event will have been registered.

Even though the family was a little upset at getting pebble-blasted, Daddy day-tripper certainly wasn't about to follow wife's insistence and confront Grub about the pebbles all over their carefully laid-out towels. Grub certainly didn't notice he'd caused any disturbance.

He trudged over to us, oblivious to the nervous sunbathers and families eyeing him like startled deer. When he reached our group, we all greeted him enthusiastically, taking in the strong aroma of Havoline and axle grease that followed him everywhere. This time there was the added nuance of probably five or six pints of scrumpy.

He pulled out a couple of bottles of wine from his leather jacket, plonked himself down on the pebbles, and proceeded to remove his boots, all the while chattering away to anyone and everyone.

Wow, the aroma quickly changed from oil and grease to sweaty Stilton, causing the nearby families who had been discreetly inching away, to up their pace, noses twitching.

Under his boots, Grub wore a pair of thick, green woollen socks, which he then also removed, swigging on one of the bottles of Chateau WoggaWogga at the same time. Under these socks, were another three layers of what one presumes were once wool, until finally, the last pair just came off in bits, revealing two lumps of flesh that looked like they'd been kept in formaldehyde for a few years. By now, our ex-neighbours were moving away as if we'd uncovered an unexploded bomb.

Thoroughly enjoying himself, and still completely oblivious of the effect he was having on the day-tripping families, Grub spots "Dave's Boat Hire" just down the beach and a big beam spreads across his face. He lurches to standing and trudges off across the beach in what was pretty much a straight line - impressive in anyone's books after more than a few pints of scrumpy, and all the more impressive due to the sinking pebbles underfoot and the obstacle course of families, deckchairs, blow up toys and tartan rugs which were hurriedly being pulled out of his path.

Twelve stone of red-haired Hell's Angel in rolled up jeans and pink legs, brandishing a bottle of red wine coming your way would certainly convince the most headstrong day-tripper to relinquish their favourite spot.

We all watched him trudging off, laughing at the trail of destruction he was un-beknowingly leaving in his wake. We soon lost sight of Grub and got back to where we were before his arrival – birdwatching and the six packs.

Some twenty minutes later, we suddenly hear this bellowing noise coming from the direction of the sea. A bit like I imagine a water buffalo might sound giving birth, we all look round. Some fifty yards out to sea is a wooden skiff, it's oars out at right angles, wobbling violently due to the large red-headed Hell's Angel doing it's best to stand upright and wave, complete with leather jacket and bottle of wine in hand.

We watched, as most of the beach were now doing, expecting, and hoping him to go over the side any moment. He eventually does lose balance, but, to our enormous disappointment he falls over backwards into the boat, two white legs sticking upwards, kicking violently. A minute or two of this goes by, then the red mop re-appears, and Grub manages to get himself into a seemingly normal sitting position, whereupon he triumphantly takes another swig from his WoggaWogga and bellows at us once more to join him.

The yelling and signalling and the excitement offered by the boat was convincing, so the three of us trogged down the beach, waded as much as possible with arms above heads then swam the last few yards to the skiff. We clambered in one by one, each time the boat getting lower in the water and tipping dangerously with each boarding. There was no doubt that the spectacle had the entire beach's attention.

How we all managed to get on board without tipping the boat over I'll never know, but with all of us in the skiff, and probably to the entire beach's disappointment, we began rowing leisurely along the water's edge some twenty or so yards out. Calm sea, blue sky, just another party of happy, normal teenagers enjoying the summer, not a care in the world

But whilst we were most definitely happy, we certainly were not normal as we had a well-oiled Grub on board. Suddendly, without warning, Grub let out a roar, dropped his half empty bottle of wine in the bottom of the boat, stands up and, fully clothed, launched himself over the side. The skiff rocked violently as if being hit by a tsunami, the three of us remaining in the boat nearly getting tipped out of the other side. By sheer luck, and with much shouting and scrambling, we managed to stay aboard. But where was Grub? He'd completely disappeared.

There we were, the three of us leaning over the sides, peering into the depths, wondering where the bloody hell Grub was. The beach audience was too, as Grub's roar and subsequent splash had regained their attention in a second.

Finally, after what seemed like an age, Grub erupts vertically out of the sea like a breaching whale, hand stretched upwards clutching a soggy pound note and yelling with jubilation.

Incredibly, he'd spotted the corner of the note about fifteen feet below, half buried in the sand, and decided to go get it. Remember a pound note would buy a couple of pints in those days.

Then it all went belly up. Grub, realizing he'd got to the sandy bottom very quickly because he'd jumped off the boat, and had only got back to the surface as he'd pushed hard upwards off the bottom, now realizes the dead-weight effect of multi-layers of soaked bike leathers and three welded motorbike chains.

He disappeared again with a drowned-out shout for help, leaving a small tidal wave and a widening circle of bubbles. With bated breath we watched again, as did the entire beach. Ten seconds later, and up shoots Grub again, only this time he'd propelled himself upwards off the bottom at an angle to get as close to the skiff as possible when he surfaced.

Even though swimming wasn't Grub's strong point he churned enough water to manage to reach the skiff. However, wet leathers, bike-chains and twelve stone of panicked Hell's Angel combined to pull the gunwale below the waterline, sure enough turning the boat immediately upside down and dumping us all in the drink.

In the mayhem, shouts and churning water we could hear the crowds on the beach roaring with laughter. I remember reaching the shore first coughing, spluttering, and trying to recover from the laughing. I was soon joined by the other two, and we turned to look for Grub, who was nowhere in sight. The rowboat was gone and so was Grub! The crowds on the beach had also now gone silent as we all just stared at the empty sea.

Then...... Excalibur!

As if by some medieval sorcery, a bottle of wine slowly appeared out of the sea surrounded by bubbles, held at the neck by an oily hand with one finger stuck in the top. The bottle and hand emerged slowly out of the waves, moving inexorably towards the shore, revealing more and more of a black leather arm as it went. Then, a foot to the right, a big soggy red blob slowly started to appear, looking like a rock covered in seaweed at low tide. Grub's head, a big grin on his face, comes into view followed, little by little, by the rest of him. His free hand was pulling the sunken boat behind him.

I can't remember hearing an entire crowd of thousands laugh so much in my life!

At that point, having seen the mayhem, Dave the boatman arrived, going absolutely mental and shouting hysterically about his wrecked boat, livelihood, poor starving children, insurance, etc., etc., He carried on shouting until he came face to face with a cross between Braveheart, a yeti and the creature from the Black Lagoon. That was Grub.

Between us, we managed to turn the boat over, empty it, and re-float it, much to Dave's relief, as this gave him an easy exit without having to press the point with Grub. Boatman Dave rowed away as fast as he could.

Back up on the beach, the dripping Grub's two main issues were the fact that his wine now had saltwater in it, and his three-chain belt would get rusty.

And, once again, we had provided first-class entertainment for the promenade.

All harmless fun.

JERSEY AND THE BANK JOB

Just before I leave the frivolities of adolescence, there is one more tale I'll include. Why, you ask?

Well, I think it's a good illustration of how the world has changed. When I was young, sure, we did stupid stuff, but it was generally harmless and looked upon as part of what growing up was all about.

The authorities, the law, the general public had a more flexible, understanding and forgiving approach to things, as you'll see. Today, everything is so much more serious, often violent, people getting prosecuted, ASBOs, all far less innocent. Pity.

Anyway, to the story.

I was around seventeen years old, and it was to be my first trip abroad, a few days' holiday in Jersey with a couple of other mates. More nutters.

Bean, a shortened form of beanpole, was over six-foot-tall, not the sharpest knife in the drawer and looked like a mop. Daley on the other hand, had a nickname coined from the then-famous TV personality, Arthur Daley, a used car salesman. Our mate Daley was one of the sharper knives, always on the make and we were sure he would, one day, be a used car salesman. Inevitable.

It was a trip we'd planned as part of our summer holidays. Jersey meant going abroad! Wow! Part of the Channel Islands, Jersey was reached via a four-hour wallow on a smelly old car ferry across the wide bit of the English Channel.

Whilst the whole trip was most definitely low budget, with the intention of winging it with bed-and-breakfast accommodation, the brochures from the travel agents promised sun-drenched beaches, golden sands and more bikini clad birds than you could ever want – which in those adolescent days, was quite a lot.

It turned out that the beaches were as sun-drenched as the BBC weather reported, which was generally grey skies and occasional drizzle. The golden sands were probably nice had there been even the faintest suggestion of a sun-drenching, and the sea certainly wasn't the Mediterranean blue the brochures purported either. It was as cold, if not colder, than our own sea back home, which wasn't surprising as it was the same English Channel.

As for the bikini clad birds, the absence of any sun-drenching and warm blue sea meant a corresponding absence of fauna. We figured they must be holed up in the many bars and teashops, so after a few valiant efforts at trying to kid ourselves we were having a good time on the deserted beaches, we gave that up and hit the town.

As was the wont of all British youngsters then and now, such trips had to involve large amounts of drinking, so most of the time was spent going from pub to pub to cheap food outlets in the vain hope of finding those ever-elusive bikini-clad girls.

Such it was, that after five days, our cash situation was becoming desperate. We didn't have credit cards in those days, and it was only the copious amounts of cheap beer that kept our spirits slightly above the "this is crap" level.

One particularly day, it was getting on for lunch time and we were sitting in some pub with an exotic name that bore little resemblance to the tatty interior, dejectedly looking at a lunch menu we couldn't afford.

The table was covered with some twenty empty bottles of flip-top Grolsch, the drizzle outside trickling down the windows and fogging up the inside panes. The inquisitive reader might wonder how come there was money for beer but not for food. Some things will never change with adolescents!

Bean came back from the bar clutching another round of liquid lunch and plonked himself down on the red, plastic bench which was covered in splits. As he popped the top of his Grolsch, Daley suddenly looked up, grinning mischievously. A look appeared on his face which suggested he'd found a tenner in his pocket. Which he hadn't.

"Letsh go rob a bank" he slurred.

We ignored him and continued staring glumly into our bottles of beer.

"Sheriush. We're in Jersey! There's loadsa banks here!"

"Yesh, Daley, we're in Jersey, an yesh, it probably does have banks.....but banks have safes. An' guards....an' Police".

"No...lishun...I've got a plan...."

It was true that the Channel Islands were supposed to be the tax haven and the offshore banking centre of the UK's rich. The place seemed sleepy enough and as we discussed, none of us remembered even seeing a policeman.

Our small group closed ranks, huddled over and began to plot. It was to be a lightning strike operation requiring detailed planning. Fortunately, the gallons of previously consumed Grolsch made things much simpler to work out, and the decision-making process that much easier. So much so that, twenty minutes later, everything had been planned down to the minutest detail and we were ready. We wobbled out of the bar, set on instant riches.

The Robbery

How we managed to get to the town centre on the rented mopeds without hitting anything is probably down to an amused St. Christopher wondering how far this would go. We stopped a couple of hundred yards down the street from the main branch of Barclays. The high street was quiet as most folks were probably having lunch.

When we arrived on the island five days previous, we had seen a fancy-dress shop not too far from where we were right now. We headed towards it, full of purpose. Three gorilla masks and three plastic water-pistols were requested, scattering several handfuls of copper coins over the glass countertop to the bemused assistant. We were convinced that the water pistols couldn't be told apart from the real thing.

I think I remember the woman in the shop asking jokingly if we were going to rob a bank, which un-nerved us slightly, but the Grolsch kept us firm.

It was time. We knew where Barclays was as we'd been in the bank across the street a couple of days earlier to change a twenty-pound note to settle some debts.

Clad in T-shirts, baggy shorts and sandals, and wearing the gorilla masks over our faces and our scooter helmets backwards to cover up our hair, we set out across the street. We must have looked like three extra-terrestrials who'd just been surfing.

Reaching the bank, we tussled our way through the revolving glass door and took up a threatening position in the bank foyer, guns out front. All three were swaying from side to side due to the Grolsh, and we had to keep our heads tilted back to stop the helmets going over our eyes. This only caused more swaying.

You are probably now questioning if this really is true. Absolutely...at least as much as I can remember.

Daley slurred in a loud.....slur "Everybody schtill. Itch a shtick up!".

In his excitement he squeezed a bit too hard on his gun trigger and a small jet of water peed out onto the floor. Why the water and not just empty guns you might ask? In our detailed planning we had decided that water-pistols full of real water were likely to receive a lesser sentence than a mock gun if any of us were captured.

Now, I do remember quite vividly, and probably because I was closest to him, the security guard, who had been sitting on a chair in the corner reading a newspaper. Big, fat fellow with glasses. He lowered the paper slightly to assess the situation. The bank was in total silence, the staff and customers remaining rigid, probably building up the breath necessary to break out into fits of laughter.

The guard coughed a little, scratched his nose, folded his paper, rose, and walked over to us. I saw him coming through my gorilla slits and defensively took a step backwards, right into Daley's puddle. I promptly went arse over tit onto my back, shooting a stream of water into the guard's crotch.

Ignoring his injuries, the guard bravely stepped over me, reached for Daley's mask and pulled it forward off his face by about a foot. Then he let it go. It slapped back onto Daley's face with a loud pop, and which no doubt stung, and Daley too went over backwards. The guard then stepped over to Bean and grabbed him by his ear.

"Now, lads – I don't know if this is a joke, or a dare or something else, but I suggest you three twerps bugger off out of here before I call the police". He then took Bean's pistol out of his hand and sent a jet of water through Bean's slits into his eyes which immediatley dribbled out from under the mask off his chin.

At that point, the entire populous of the bank burst out laughing.

Making a tactical decision to retreat from the floor, I tried to get up a couple of times, beaten by the slippery wet marble. I eventually managed to reach the revolving door on all fours, closely followed by a dripping Bean and a blind Daley, whose mask was completely out of line with his features and was squirting water in all directions, doing his best to depart in a squirt of glory as the Sundance Kid no doubt would have done.

The guard rolled his eyes as we left, probably a little annoyed at being interrupted, but more than likely quite amused by the whole affair.

To cut a long story short, we legged it to the scooters and whizzed off, weaving our way to the nearest beach to hide in the dunes and escape the posse.

I've included this episode just to show how the world has changed. Imagine doing that now?

The Golden Earring

Just to finish the story, our last night on Jersey arrived, and yes, we were looking forward to getting home.

Even though it had been a damp week, I must admit it hadn't all been doom and gloom. We had managed to spend some time on the beach and generally a reasonable time was had by all. The headaches from the bank job had subsided swiftly, as they do in young folks, and it came to our final night. A real blow out was in order!

I'll now jump directly to the next morning, prior to leaving for the ferry terminal.

We'd woken up – just about – in a cheap B&B. I'd lost my jacket, which contained my house keys, ferry ticket, and passport, so I was in a right state as it was midday and the ferry was leaving at 3pm. I remember that I had been wearing my jacket the previous night, so we set out to find it.

We decided the police station would be the last resort in case news of an attempted bank robbery had gotten out.

Uncertain of where we actually had been, we decided to start at the first pub in St. Brelades and work our way up along the bars. I also had a strange bruise on my face. Not a good sign.

On entering, the barman confirmed that he did indeed remember us from the night before but had not found any jacket.

"I'm sure you left wearing it " he told us in a dis-interested voice. This obviously wasn't the first time it had happened.

We continued to the next bar, asking the same question. Same response. The process continued three or four more times, each time the reception becoming a little more hostile.

Finally, we arrived at the last bar in the main street. As soon as we entered, the barman scowled, asking what we wanted. I enquired about a black jacket.

"You left carrying it, on your way to The Golden Earring".

"To where?" I asked.

"The Golden Earring. Club up the alley way, you went there after here, 'cos we were closing, and we chucked you out. We told you to go there as it was the only place nearby that stayed open late."

"Ah, great, thanks!" We were relieved we were finally getting somewhere.

Sure enough, up the alley was a sign The Golden Earring, and a doorway leading into the club. Luckily, the door was open as they were re-stocking the bar. Inside, dark, and the smell that only a seedy nightclub has the following day.

A bloke was behind the bar, cleaning glasses. As soon as we walked in, he looked up at us and, after a moment of recognition, said dangerously

"You've got a bloody nerve coming back in here!"

"Oops, bugger, here we go."

The barman then proceeded to tell us what had happened, as had been well beyond remembering. Apparently, we'd arrived in the Golden Earring gay club about eleven thirty, three good looking seventeen-year old's blindly in search of the sun-drenched bikini clad girls that had been eluding us all week.

Apparently, we had been too pissed to notice the hundred or so Village People lookalikes in black leathers and tight Tee-shirts drooling like wild prairie dogs as if dinner had just been served.

Having got a round of drinks from the bar, we were still completely oblivious to the fact that there wasn't a single female in the place and innocently (drunkenly more like) putting the frequent arse-grabbing down to a tightly packed house.

Propping up the bar, it wasn't long before a large, fat, but muscular bloke came over, dressed in a New York cop uniform. He literally picked me up and carried me in a bear-hug onto the dance floor for a slow dance.

Up to then I really hadn't much of a clue what was going on, but at this point animal instincts suddenly overrode the effects of the beer and I twigged. Thank God I did, as the big, fat face with a Freddy Mercury moustache was moving in, tongue out for a big sloppy smacker, both hands firmly gripping my buttocks.

As I was completely immobilized in the thing's grip, I don't know if it was the panic or the bear-hug, but the only thing I could do in response to his amorous advance was to release approximately nine pints of Flip-top Grolsch from my gut straight into his face at a pressure that would have made his fireman friend proud.

The face disappeared in a brown explosion, diced carrots, the lot. He immediately dropped me, recoiled backwards desperately trying to wipe the puke from his eyes, bits of prawn korma dripping off his once-splendid Freddy moustache. His next move was downwards, as he lost all traction on the already slippery dance floor, crashing down on his backside in vomit. His third action was to recover, get back on his feet, and punch me square in the mush.

Then all hell broke loose. Daley and Bean, fuelled by our good friend Grolsch, and crying with laughter, were over like a couple of spaniels to support yours truly. Freddy's shemale buddies, fireman, Indian and construction worker joined in, as did the barman who leapt over the counter wielding a telescopic baton. The last I remember was seeing the bouncers moving in.

We're now back to where I left off the following morning. After recounting the events the owner now had a smirk on his face.

"I have to admit, the look on Old Blue Eyes' face when you honked on him was bloody hysterical. By the way, your jacket's over there. Quick drink before your go?"

Whilst this was another tale of adolescent mischief, it was, as said before, innocent fun and in a way almost accepted. No police, no arrests, no knives, no community service and generally, no hard feelings.

The world has, however, changed.

Unfortunately, I don't think I did.

THE POPE

In 1983, Pope John Paul came to visit Canterbury, where I was at university. Even though it was a major event not just for the City but for the whole country, I wasn't particularly interested.

Not being even slightly religious in those times, my only attempts at communication with Him of Upstairs were generally limited to the times when I hoped my hand would beat the other bloke's or in the request for assistance in getting rid of the headache.

The Pope's visit was quite frankly a pain in the ass, mainly because the whole city was in lock-down. The preparations had been going on for weeks, with the build-up gripping the whole city.

For the actual visit, His Popeness was apparently going to drive through the City Centre in his Pope Mobile, do something holy in the Cathedral, meet some dignitaries, maybe play a round of three-card brag with some students (only joking!) and then return to London leaving the whole city gasping in ecstacy.

Canterbury was heaving. Tens of thousands of people were crammed into the Cathedral grounds and every street within the city walls. They lined every inch of the intended route through the city centre. They'd been there from before dawn, and apparently folks had come from across the country to see Him.

I, on the other hand, was minding my own business, just leaving the campus with a definite "morning after" feel and smell, heading towards a corner shop for some Lucozade and painkillers. I was keeping as far away as possible from the excitement. I wandered through Lady Wooten's Green, arriving at the main ring-road that encircles Canterbury, paralleling its ancient walls. I looked and felt like shit.

Anyway, I came to a zebra crossing and moronically pressed the "cross" button even though there wasn't a car in sight. All of a sudden, a couple of police motorcycles, blue lights flashing, roared around the corner, and screeched to a halt in front of me, almost knocking me over. One of the riders dismounted.

"Shit" I thought, "I'm sure she told me she was eighteen…..".

One of the coppers lifted up his visor, and politely said "Excuse me, Sir. Would you mind waiting here for a moment?"

Whilst I tried to digest the fact I wasn't being arrested and had just been called "Sir", it appeared. The Pope-Mobile, sedately coming around the corner straight towards me.

On it's own.

The strange vehicle, which looked like a large, rounded fish-tank on a golf cart approached with non other than his Popeness himself, sitting calmly aloof and isolated in his mobile aquarium. The head of the driver was just visible at the front, much lower down.

As it approached the crossing, the vehicle slowed down to an almost complete stop right there in front of me. Apart from the two police officers, who were busy looking out for any suspicious anti-Pope-like activity and keeping a wary eye on me, I was the only one there. His Holiness stopped in his fish tank and looked down at me standing there on the pavement looking back up at Him.

Can you imagine the scene? A miserably boring and empty concrete ring-road, a grubby git standing on the kerb at a zebra crossing, two police bikers and the Pope Mobile with a real live Pope inside it? Stopped.

Now, as my head wasn't exactly clear, I automatically assumed he was respecting the highway code as any good driver should and letting me cross. I didn't know if I should set forth, or wave him on. The Pope gave me a broad grin, and waved, maybe cheered by the fact that at least one bloke had bothered to turn out to greet him in Canterbury.

I smiled and waved back. I don't think he realized I was waving him on, but his smile broadened further, and waving as only such exalted persons can, he trundled by.

The two police outriders were then gone in a flash, and a few seconds later the rest of the Pope entourage in big cars came around the corner to catch up.

OK, so technically, I didn't actually meet Him, but we had a moment. And even though I was a non-believer, I can tell you it was quite profound. I seem to recall my headache had receded. To this day, I am sure that he must have remembered me and during some divine future conference, put in a good a word with St. Christopher.

Before I move on, I'll mention that just prior to His arrival at the Cathedral, there had been a gas leak, or some such scare and He had been re-routed around the city walls, much to the disappointment of all the people who had been patiently waiting for him for days.

I actually met the Pope again in later life, but that's another story.

FAST COURIER

After surviving three years of mayhem and debauchery at University, with only God knowing how I managed to get an Honour's Degree, I was faced with the challenge of most graduates. "Now what? Oh shit – the fun's over! Better start looking for a job."

As was then, and as is today, unless you were an academic star with a First, or you have a double-barrelled name, or your old man had contacts, once you've worn the silly robe and hat, shaken the Dean's hand - who's some old codger you've never seen before - and got the scroll in some excruciatingly embarrassing ceremony to which your parents insist on coming and meeting your friends, the majority of whom should be in prison, you go out and look for a job.

Remember, Internet wasn't around back then so it was all newspaper classifieds and telephones, a depressingly tedious task. Even though Uni had been sold to me as the guarantee to employment and stardom, it certainly wasn't like that in my case, and I was basically after any job I could find.

From what I hear, it's even more acute these days as there are now five million universities in the UK chucking out God knows how many poorly prepared individuals to the non-existent labour market every June.

Plastic Pipes and Valves

Lo and behold, I was fortunate enough to land a job quickly, working for a large company in London which manufactured plastic pipes and valves. Exciting stuff and exactly what I'd spent three years studying Geography and Art for!

Anyway, I stuck it out for almost two years. No interest whatsoever, job satisfaction zero, no prospects, weekly disappointment at the meager pay-packet which had all been spent before I'd even got it. Fortunately, credit cards were a thing of both novelty and exclusivity, so I didn't fall into the debt trap that a lot of folks do these days.

So, almost twenty-four months working my arse off nine-to-five in a shitty office-come-factory in North East London, Angel Islington to be precise.

Bored out of my mind, day in, day out, complete drudgery, I had absolutely no interest in what I was doing. On top of that, I was living in a crappy, over-priced rented room in Enfield, with a lunatic landlord who had a fetish for replacing the roof of the house once a year, usually in January. I remember a good-sized chunk of my pay went every month on that rat-infested dive.

How many folks live like that and never get out of it? I think it was those initial years which made me set on taking a different path.

I began in the Plastic Pipe and Valve exhibition department, which I must admit did offer the odd entertaining moment, mainly from the lunatcs with whom I worked. Curiously enough, I was ignorant to the fact that those early days were sowing the seeds for a future venture.

As I seemed to be a reliable bloke (those are about all the words of encouragement I remember ever getting) I was promoted in the second year to sales engineer.

Wow! "Promoted" however, sounds a lot more majestic than it really was. In that company there were bosses and grunts and I was most definitely a grunt and as things looked, would most likely always be one.

On the bright side, the new job offered the same pay, but with a chance of commission from going out on the road wearing a cheap suit and tie and selling...yes... plastic valves and pipes!

Trying to convince the country's leading Plastic Pipe and Valve users, usually found in some dingy workshop in east London to buy my products, with me not knowing the first thing about plastic pipes and valves, was about as interesting to me as....well...plastic pipes!

My total lack of conviction and knowledge of my products was sniffed out by the buyers as soon as I came in through the door, and these folks were not the most amiable of people.

As you can imagine, the monthly commission on sales wouldn't have bought me a pint. I endured this new job for a month, then decided that was it. I walked out, went home, packed up my stuff, and left Enfield for good.

My girlfriend of the time was living in Ealing, so that's where I headed.

And here comes lesson-in-life number two. A boyfriend's attraction to his girlfriend takes on a whole new light when unemployed boyfriend suddenly pitches up on girlfriend's step looking for a place to doss. I needed another job, onto-bloody-pronto or I would be very soon be an "ex". I was given a week.

A day or two later, sitting in a café with a mug of tea and a copy of the Evening Standard, I saw an advertisement in the classifieds for Fast Courier.

"Hmmm…a courier driver?" I thought, slightly excited by the idea, having had plenty of exposure to this special breed of wheeled lunatic in the previous job.

I reckon I could handle that. Plus, I didn't have a car and driving was still a novelty, remembering that the laws on Her Majesty's highways in those days were far more relaxed than today. Speed cameras didn't exist, and you could have more than a thimble-full of beer and still legally drive.

I called the Courier company and was gruffly invited by a certain Bill to go around to the depot the following day.

The Tax Inspector

Now, I'm not sure about you, but if I go for a job interview, I wear a suit and tie, unless it's for a barman in Aruba, or to be a suicide bomber. So, all togged up, I took the tube to Heathrow and then as a short-cut had to walk across a freshly ploughed field towards a small industrial estate where Fast Courier was based.

Now, these industrial estates dotted around the outskirts of London are not nice places. At all.

Rubbish all over the place, rusty cars, piles of rubble, peeling paint, tatty signs flapping in the wind, lots of chains and padlocks, signs telling you to beware of the dog or get mauled to death, lots of crappy vans, all windows barred, cracked glass, gaping black open garage doors with evil smells and sounds coming from within.

These places were populated by people who would have easily gotten supporting roles in the Book of Eli or Mad Max, and that's without the need for wardrobe or make-up. Not folks you want to mess with or places you want to be at night.

I spotted a faded, hand-painted sign on the side of a corrugated tin-roofed warehouse that told me I had found Fast Courier. The angle at which the sign was tilted and about to come away from the wall also told me that Fast Courier obviously invested their maintenance money elsewhere.

I trudged past a barred and dirty window, still trying to scrape the mud off my shoes. As I came to a second filthy window, I could just make out through the muck what appeared to be a dingy office with a desk, a filing cabinet and an enormous fat bloke sitting behind it talking into a microphone.

Bill, perhaps? As I peered in, he looked up and saw me.

I looked away and entered the lock-up, passing by a rusty blue door to what looked like and smelt like the toilet, presumably for the drivers. My nervous gaze fell on a few filthy plastic chairs, a pile of old porno magazines and newspapers, an over-flowing plastic bin and not much else, except for stacks of cardboard boxes with labels.

A door was visible in the dim interior with "Office" on a hand-painted sign. Fast Couriers' nerve centre! Apart from that the place was deserted.

I knocked on the office door. Nothing.

I knocked again. Nothing.

Well, I knew he was in there. Maybe he's using headphones? So, I went in.

Empty. "Very odd. Where the fuck's fat Bill? He didn't pass me coming in" I thought.

I stood for a moment hearing voices on the radio, and then heard a shuffling noise from behind the desk. I stepped forward and looked over it and there was fat man, flat on his back on the floor, looking up at me.

"Er...Hello" I said, a little uncertain. "I'm here about the job".

"What?" said Bill, looking up at me, still flat on his back, red faced and a gob of spittle dribbling out of his mouth.

"The drivers' job? We spoke on the phone yesterday? I'm Jack."

"Why you dressed like that"? growled Bill, his puce face now turning to a threatening scowl.

Not too sure of myself, I said "Well, it's a job interview."

"You shit-head, I fort you was from the fuckin' Inland fuckin' Revenue. Only them twats dress like that round 'ere".

At this, Bill started going through several intermediate positions and with enormous effort, managed to get himself off the floor and flopped back into the shabby swivel chair. On his back, he reminded me of an up-ended turtle.

The radio crackled.

"Bill, John 'ere, all done in Putney, my son!"

Bill waved his flabby hand at me to sit on a small cabinet, skated over to the control board and pressed the transmit button.

"Nice one, Knocker, come on back in and leave the van. That's it for today. Be 'ere early tumorruh."

Bill then looked back at me and we just stared at each other, an obvious lack of understanding from both parties on what exactly each was looking at.

"Let's see yer licence" he said.

I passed it over. After a very quick glance, he said " When can you start?"

"Errr…straight away, I suppose" I replied.

"Good, see that pile of boxes out there in the shop, the address is on one of 'em. Take the white Escort out there in the yard." He pointed at the office wall, presumably in the same direction the van was to be found.

"Call in – ere's the number - when yer done. Oh, an' when you drop the gear off, make sure they sign this receipt for the same number of boxes. Goddit? Ere's the keys....and here's the docket. They sign 'ere." A grubby stub stabbed the docket.

"We pay one-sixty an hour, time starts when I see yer face in the mornin' an' finishes when you done yer last drop. Any problems with the law, that's your problem."

And with that, he flung a set of car keys at me and got back to shuffling the paperwork on his desk.

"Err...I meant tomorrow.....I can start tomorrow".

He cut me off. "Listen, mate, in this business now is now. Fast Courier means fucking fast. Got it? So? You want the job or not?"

"Err...Yes!" I said,

"Right. Now fuckin' move. I'll be 'ere when you get back to lock up, so don't dilly-fuckin'-dally. An yer might like to lose the poofy fuckin' tie!"

At which point he grinned at his razor-sharp wit and got back to his paper shuffling.

I went outside, yanked off my tie, shrugged out of my jacket and looked at the address on the first box.

The madness starts

Erith? Erith! You must be bloody joking! I'm close to Heathrow, and Erith is on the other side of London, just by Dartmouth, and it's almost rush hour! It'll take hours to get there. I went outside looking for a white Escort van and saw a beat-up piece of shit that looked like it had never been washed in all it's years of misuse.

Half bald tyres, more scrapes and dents than you can imagine, and dirty? The cab floor and dashboard was littered with cigarette stubs, other stubs, empty take-away cartons, the odd, blackened banana skin, an assortment of empty cans and old Sun newspapers. It was disgusting.

And that is when my education into courier driving started. Anyone who has driven as a courier will know. They live in a different world. It's all about speed at all costs and no costs at all costs. Traffic is an obstacle course, a challenge to be dealt with, pavements are extensions of roadways, yellow lines mean nothing, red lights are to stop other traffic while you go through, courier motorcycles were targets to be taken out. Absolute mayhem.

You ate fast, on the go, a street map on your lap, a can of beer or paper mug of tea, bantering on the radio with Fat Bill and the others, no stopping. No GPS in those days, no smartphones. It was maps, your own wits, hell for leather, taking risks, avoiding the law and above all, enormous fun. At least it was at the beginning.

I managed the Erith initiation and I think Bill was quietly impressed when I got back about three hours later.

"You're back early. Wot 'appened?" expecting me to start with the excuses.

"Nothin'" I said, starting to adapt to the language "'ere's the dockit. No worries".

Bill took it off me and looked up. " Err….right, good….be 'ere tumorruh at six" and dismissed me by returning to his papers.

I suspect he was already thinking to himself "This bloke's a fucking nutter and he's only just started!"

Next morning, around six am, I met most of Fast Couriers' other drivers. The word "driver" is far too complimentary for this lot. It soon became apparent I was working with the biggest bunch of cowboys, maniacs, addicts, crooks, shysters and con artists this side of, well, Erith. We'd all meet up in the mornings, generally reeking of the night before, half of them (us) probably still way over the legal limit, and get our rounds assigned by Fat Bill.

Curiously, the industrial unit next door to Fast Courier distributed sex toys. They had a rubbish skip out front where they dumped all the rejects. Nice!

One of our fellas, Alex, would arrive at six in the morning, fall out of his Transit with smoke billowing out of the cab, the joint still hanging out of his mouth. He'd clock in, get his assignments, load up and, before setting off, would then jump into next door's skip to see what goodies were to be had.

Five minutes of rummaging later, he'd clamber back out clutching half a dozen sex toys, ranging from dolls to rubber dildos, bung them onto the front seat of the Transit and speed out of the compound. As he departed, he'd be whooping like a red Indian, hanging out of the still open Transit door and waving a sabre in the air – yes, a real Hussar's sabre – the joint still hanging out of his mouth.

At this, Fat Bill would come running out of the office brandishing a .22 repeating air pistol, shooting as many slugs at the receding Alex as possible, whilst me and the other drivers would cheer them on. This was good fun. These blokes where complete bloody nutters, every one of them.

Alex told me the sabre was "insurance in case of any agro…". Wow! His favourite trick was to wait at traffic lights until a car would pull up alongside driven by a woman with an open window – or even better, an open top. He'd then select a big, black rubber dildo or something similarly lewd and lob it onto her lap. For him, this was the best fun in the world, and I know for a fact that not all the recipients of these pranks were upset. Not sure it would go down well in today's PC world.

Working for Fast Courier was an education into the black world of hard work, on the edge, no rules and no labour laws to protect you. You didn't like it, then piss off! I worked generally from six till six, and occasionally on Saturday mornings, most often out of the cargo "horseshoe" at Heathrow. Often, you'd get home very late if some emergency job came up. For this, I netted around a hundred pounds a week, which at £1.60 an hour, was diabolical, even in 1989.

To my credit, when I left, I was the top driver, on average making 90% of the daily drops, basically due to good route planning, meaning that as soon as I had been given my drops in the morning, I'd go and get a cuppa from a nearby tea wagon and sit in the van for half an hour working out the most efficient route with my A to Z. These days there are no doubt route efficiency APP's and GPS for this.

Whilst it was initially great fun, and many outrageous stories I could tell, I soon realized that Fast Courier was a fast road to nowhere and things would have to change, otherwise I'd wind up like the sabre-wielding, dildo-chucking crack-head Alex.

So, how did I get out? One day I had to deliver a box of catalogues to a mobile exhibition unit in Camber Sands. I arrived much earlier than expected, which surprised the client enormously, so he offered me a coffee and we struck up a conversation. A week later, I started in the exhibition game.

I found out later that three weeks after I left, Fast Courier went bankrupt. The owner had been discovered with a pallet of cocaine in his lounge and got ten years. The police obviously raided the depot and half the drivers were done for one felony or another.

Saved by the bell!

THE FEAR OF FLYING

Aviophobia is, according to Wikipedia, the official term for the fear of flying. And I suffer from it, which is rather strange as I am not really afraid of heights. I've parachuted out of an airplane, stood on the edge of a two-thousand-foot cliff edge and looked down, no worries. Weird.

My particular brand of aviophobia, however, is a little different. I'm not afraid of all aircraft, only the big ones with four hundred people packed in, sitting on top of one-hundred and fifty tons of high-octane jet fuel, when I'm cramped in the back in toilet class. Business class eases the anxiety somewhat, the space and the free hooch helping significantly.

Small planes, however, I have no problem with at all. I've flown in an open-cockpit Tiger Moth, flown upside down above a racing circuit trying to beat a Fiat Touring car, done aerobatics in a Pitts Special over Key West and flown onto oil rigs in helicopters in 100km/hr winds to name just a few, and loved it. But strap me in a fully loaded Jumbo Jet with five hundred other dudes and I shit myself.

So, the smaller the aircraft, the happier I am. Psychologists would probably say it's something to do with being in control or having the ability to influence your destiny if the pilot has a heart attack. I'd tend to agree, it's all about self-control or the lack of not being in control.

There were two times when I flew when I was actually in total control from start to finish. Well, almost. Once was dangling on the end of a parachute, and the other hanging below a paraglider.

The Parachutist

My parachuting experience took place in Nantwich, close to Chester. Something I'd always wanted to do, I signed up for a short course and a jump. Although I envisaged myself freefalling for thousands of feet and doing all the skydiving acrobatics, the first step was a much more mundane affair which all first timers go through. The static line jump.

A very low risk event, you spend a few hours on the ground, going through the motions of how to land, how to roll, how to take the impact, how to look at the wind direction, how to control the basic 'chutes direction and most importantly what to do if the bloody parachute doesn't open. I listened hard to that bit.

In the afternoon, the weather was good enough, so the novice group of a dozen or so folks of all shapes and creeds, old and young, cocky and nervous, all chattering excitedly piled into the plane through the open door at the back, which in fact wasn't door at all. It was just a big square hole.

The plane started up, rumbled along the grass and with a roar from the engine and a few bumps we quickly became airborne. The sound of the engine was quickly drowned out by the howling wind rushing past the gaping door.

The nervous laughing of the group had now gone. There were now a lot of very anxious looking faces all staring nervously at the open door, the same thing going through everyone's mind …that there was no going back now!

The instructor soon gives a yell and tells everybody to line up. He then clips everyone's static line to the overhead cable fixed parallel to the plane's roof. This means that on going out of the door, the novice simply plummets earthwards whilst the static line does all the rest, deploys the chute and novice floats safely and serenely to the ground.

And that's exactly what happened. As I was Mr. Gung-ho, I was first to go and I waddled towards the hatch, grabbed the edges and the Instructor yelled "GO!" and slapped me on the back.

I wasn't nervous, didn't hesitate, just launched myself into thin air. Strange for a bloke who's scared of flying, no? The blur of suddenly being hit by the airstream and plummeting downwards was suddenly halted as the static line did its job, the chute opened, and everything slowed to a stop and I was suddenly floating serenely above the Cheshire countryside.

The whole descent only took three or four minutes, but it seemed like eternity. It was magical. Breath-taking. And there was Mr. Aviophobia, dangling a couple of thousand feet above the ground suspended only by a few nylon cords. Explain that.

My reverie was soon interrupted as the approaching ground started to come up faster and faster. As I was so certain that I would be landing where I was supposed to land, and had admittedly lost concentration enjoying the descent, I had forgotten to pay much attention to the landing zone, and more importantly look at the windsock. If you don't land into wind, you'll have to do pretty good impression of Usain Bolt on landing or fall flat on your face and get dragged along by the chute.

Seeming expertly, some forty or fifty feet off the ground, I pulled on the appropriate riser, the chute swiveled around, and I then flared and dropped onto both feet as if I had just stepped off a chair. Didn't even fall over or even need to take a step. I could hear applause! Feeling like a pro, I started to gather in the chute as it slowly collapsed and watched my fellow jumpers land. I don't know if it was the nervous reaction of having finally done it, but as each one landed, tumbled over, got dragged face-first along the ground or did the Usain Bolt, I simply couldn't stop laughing. I laughed till I cried. I'm going to do this again.

There was one small problem though. I am an impatient git who likes to move up the ladder of progess pretty damn quick. So, when they told me that before I would be allowed to leap freely out of a plane from ten thousand feet on a Snowboard and skydive acrobatically with twenty other free-fallers, I'd have to do a few more static line jumps. Hmm, not good. I needed something more exciting now.

So, I went paragliding.

The Paraglider

The difference between the static line parachute jump and paragliding, or para-ascending as some call it, is significant. The parachute canopy as used by novices is a bloody great nylon hemispherical dome, with two control lines and you basically go down without doing anything. That's it. You can swivel around and flare but basically, it's a one-way drift. Downwards.

Paragliding on the other hand is a whole different ball game. For starters, the chute is a big, rectangular wing. Made of nylon, it inflates itself with the rush of air below and you can control it a lot more, steering any which way you want. You can even make tight circles such that you find yourself higher than the wing itself. Sure, that's for the experts who go in search of thermals and can spend hours flying. Still, I'd done my static line parachute jump....!

The paragliding school I went to was somewhere in the South Downs near London. Flights were launched from the top of one of the hills. As there was no ledge to jump off and the canopy wing needs moving air to inflate itself, you stand up in the harness with the wing spread out on the ground behind you and then start running down the slope. The canopy starts to fill and rise behind you and eventually has enough power to lift you airborne. And off you go, picked up in a small canvas chair to soar with the birds and enjoy the view. Flying in its purest sense.

I had signed up for a weekend's introductory course and after an hour's basic coaching which was focused mainly on how to control the canopy and how to land safely, the group of eager novices assembled at the top of a fairly steep sloping hill, which got even steeper as you went further down.

During instruction we had experienced the filled canopy above our heads and felt it's force but we never actually left the ground. Forward movement is needed for that.

As usual, I was selected to go first, probably because I exuded a false sense of confidence and was also the village idiot. Plus, I think the instructors suspected that in such practical matters, I was probably pretty capable. So, there I stood, harness checks done, big yellow canopy spread out behind me, the wind slight but threatening to fill it at any time. The instructor made the final check, gave me the thumbs up and pointed down the hill. "Go!".

Off I went at full pelt, which was completely un-necessary, as a fast walk would have been enough. Must have been the adrenalin, but I went for it at full tilt. The canopy filled almost immediately and suddenly the running was getting harder and harder as the wing pulled back and upwards. Then, by magic, my feet left the ground and I up I went. Yeehaa!

It was great, sitting in the little seat, soaring like an eagle, taking in the stunning view. I could see other canopies all around, small, coloured dots seemingly miles above. As I left the ground everything seemed to go into slow motion. The ground was no longer rushing beneath my feet, there was no shouting. It was all quiet. Totally serene.

As I was no expert and this was a basic canopy, I was in fact still going downwards at a fairly brisk rate of descent, but the fact that the hill was going down at a similar rate kept me airborne, probably only about a hundred feet off the ground at the highest point of the flight. However, it seemed much higher.

After what must have been only two or three minutes, the hill beneath me stopped being a hill and became a flat field. This meant that me, still descending fast, was now on collision course with planet earth and should be getting ready for the imminent landing. Unfortunately, though, I was enjoying myself so much that not only was I unaware of the speed of the approaching ground, but I also wasn't paying attention to the windsock.   Some folks never learn.

Someone shouting below me snapped me back to reality and, about thirty feet off the deck, I looked down and noticed that I was landing with the wind behind me. "Oh shit!" as Usain Bolt came immediately to mind!

At that altitude, it was too late to turn back into wind, so, travelling at some twenty-five miles an hour, with twenty miles an hour of wind behind, I was coming in at around forty five miles an hour.

I started running in mid-air, more like panic-driven peddling actually, as sprinting is not as easy as it sounds when you're sitting in a canvas chair with your arms above your head. As I came in, my little legs were probably managing no more than a meagre ten miles an hour, meaning there was thirty-five mile an hour deficit to be made up. My feet hit the ground, immediately folded backwards underneath me and I went face down at forty-five miles an hour across the landing zone.

The landing zone was in fact a bog-standard cow field. As it was early spring, and probably because of the paragliding there were no actual cattle at that time, but out there bordering the cleared landing area, there was an abundance of evidence that the herd had only recently left and had done a whole lot of cud-chewing before doing so.

So, Biggles comes hurtling in, face down a forty-five miles an hour, traverses the landing zone in milliseconds and ploughs head-first through cow-pat alley. Big black one's, the size of frying pans, the pats were a thin crust on the outside, but still lovely and moist on the inside. There was nothing I could do apart from hang on for dear life, keep eyes and mouth shut and hope it stopped soon. Which it did, but only after having been dragged about fifty yards and a hundred cow-pats, face first, until finally the canopy folded, and I came to a halt.

I staggered to my feet, my face and upper body looking like .... well.... frankly speaking... shat out of a cow. The instructor and several others came running up, their faces of concern immediately disappearing as they exploded into guffaws of laughter at the sight of me with goo dripping off my chin and about ten inches of cow dung piled on top of my head.

Trying to muster as much self-aplomb as possible, I wiped off as best I could, scooped up the canopy, and began the long haul back up the hill for a second run. News had obviously been radioed ahead as everyone at the top, especially the instructor, was laughing as 'shithead', arrived.

That afternoon, I made quite a few more jumps, and generally had a great time, but feeling very envious of the pros who didn't have to march up the bloody mountain each time. They were able to land where they had taken off, and certainly didn't stink of cow shit. One day I'll be there.

The day finished with a girl who wasn't in our group breaking her back as her canopy folded at ninety feet. There's always a sting.

Didn't I say I don't like flying if I am not in control? Whatever, but what I do now know is that Fondant de Chocolate will never be the same again!

THE OLD MAN AND THE TRAIN

I decided to include this little anecdote mainly because it involved several members of my family. The main character, however, is my Grandad, on my mother's side, a man for whom I had unbounded respect and admiration.

Percy – the discreet hero

Percy was a wonderful man, a typical Manchester working-class bloke of the day, working on the railways. When the Second World war came, he enlisted to defend his country, and left with a rifle in his hand to fight alongside the Ghurkas in Burma. This was a particularly savage theatre of conflict against the Japanese.

He came back five years later, alive, un-injured, at least physically, to his wife and daughter who had survived the Manchester bombings and five years of hardship. In his later years, even when pressed, Percy spoke little of his wartime experiences. He just showed us his Kukri, a curved Gurka knife he had been given, and his collection of medals.

Looking at him as an old, kind man, you simply can't imagine what he and millions of others like him had been through. Discreet heroism.

Our Grandmother, his wife of almost sixty years had died a couple of years earlier after a long illness, leaving Percy on his own and without his soulmate.

Not having much money, he had to sell their house to pay for a care-home, which backed on to a particularly scruffy housing estate in Exeter.

I remember visiting, walking with him in the park, and hearing the kids of the day, youngsters, swearing and cursing, pissing against the trees, showing no respect for anyone. This is what he had fought for?

Percy died an ignominious and lonely death in 1995 in hospital in Devon. My mother was not happy with the nursing home where he had been living – sorry, existing – so she planned to move him nearer to where she lived. However, before these could be implemented, the old fellow became ill and probably just gave up. None of the family were informed in time, as we were all in different corners of the world and instantaneous communications weren't around then. He passed away before any of us had a chance to say goodbye.

I am still affected by this more than twenty-five years later, and when I see the way modern society of today is going, and think back of men like Percy who fought and died to protect a country and it's values of that time, I despair.

Anyway, to the story. A few years prior to Percy's death, my brother was living in Assen, a small town in the northern part of Holland. Fans of motorcycle racing will have heard of Assen, as it is a big event on the annual racing calendar, when the small, quaint town of some fifty-thousand board up their windows and play host to one hundred thousand bikers for a long weekend of mayhem.

As a surprise for his birthday, Mum and I decided to take Percy to Assen. Not to the biker's event, but in late summer, when it was quiet and not so hot. Apart from going to Burma on a troopship in 1940, Percy had never been abroad, so we thought that a little holiday would do him good, especially as he had never been in a modern jet aeroplane.

Dutch Trains

On the big day, we helped Percy pack his suitcase and knot his tie; a whole life of discipline would never allow him to set foot outside the house unless he had a tie on. We got a taxi up to Heathrow to fly to Schipol, Amsterdam's international airport. There, Bro would collect us and drive the one hundred and fifty kilometers up through central Holland.

The journey out was trouble free, all of us having a great week at my brother's, especially Percy who spent most of the time with his great grandchildren.

The time to depart came all too quickly, and as Bro was working that day, Percy, Mum and I were to take the train back to Schipol, where the train terminal is conveniently below the airport. Percy couldn't walk very far at all.

We said our goodbyes, boarded the train directly from Assen, and were to arrive at the airport around six in the evening, giving us plenty of time to shuffle up the platform to the lifts and check-in, shuffling being the maximum speed Percy could achieve with his eighty-plus years.

As the train slowed to a halt under the airport, we waited for it to come to a complete stop before standing up, as any jerk could have sent Percy tumbling. I was to look after the suitcases while Mum assisted her Dad.

Now at a standstill, the doors of the carriage hissed opened automatically. What we didn't know was that they were on a timer and consequently would also close automatically.

The plan was for Mum to get off first, find a luggage trolley and I would then help Percy and the bags down onto the platform. It's amazing when you have small children or old folks how every little event needs a higher level of forward planning!

Anyway, Mum disembarked and went in search of the trolley. I told Percy to sit and wait whilst I started hefting the bags off the train. It was two steps down, so I had to get off and back on the train for each bag. With the third case safely on the platform, I came back for Percy, who was having a bit of an old man's moment with his coat, trying to put it on back to front. I tugged it off him, turned it round and just as he was about to put the first arm in, there was a distant whistle, then a nearby hiss as the train's doors began to close.

I looked around in panic in the hope for help, but the one or two passengers were ensconced in newspapers. Almost imperceptibly, the train started to move. I couldn't let go of Percy in case he toppled, so I stood helplessly and gesticulated at Mum slipping by down on the platform with a luggage trolley, three heavy suitcases and a look of panic on her face.

"Don't Panic Mr. Mannering!" even though panic was most definitely the order of the moment. Even though Mum was a well-travelled lady, being left on a platform in a foreign country on her own, three heavy bags to take care of and her travelling companions disappearing into a tunnel when our flight was soon to leave, there was no doubt she wasn't a happy camper by the look on her face as we disappeared from view.

Back on the train, it was almost complete silence. Dutch trains are very quiet.

"Well, Grandad" I said as nonchalantly as possible "Now we're in the poo - we'll soon be in the centre of Amsterdam, and your daughter's back there. With the bags. And the passports. And the money".

Today, I would have reached for the mobile phone. None back then.

Fortunately, whilst I was trying to decide on the best course of action, the train's ticket-collector came into the carriage and who, as do all Dutchmen, spoke a good amount of English. I asked for help.

"Yarr Meneer, next storp, duh train will storp in duh place of industry. You get orf du train dare, pass frew a tur-nel and take duh train back".

He then produced a timetable, informing us that the return train would take us back to Schipol after just a two-minute wait in the industrial zone station. Hmm, at Percy's pace, it would be tight.

Meanwhile, back on the Platform at Schipol, Mum was probably panicking and rousing the Police, the Fire-brigade, the National Guard, and probably the Prime

Minister would have been alerted. There was no way for us, however, to contact her.

After about ten minutes of going further away from Mum, the train began to slow as it a approached the Industry station. Now knowing what to expect, I was taking no chances this time, and hastily started preparing Percy for a swift exit, propelling him slowly towards the doors, knowing that our time for escape was limited.

With the train about to come to a halt, Percy pipes up. "Jack, lad, I could do with the toilet quite soon."

"Oh shit! Not now!" I thought as anyone who has any experience of old folks' needs, "soon" pretty much means now.

The doors open, and I literally carry Percy down off the train onto the platform, wildly glancing in all directions in search of the tunnel to the other platform and a toilet. My initial thought was "Tunnel first, then bog!"

"Where's the bloody tunnel?" I'm screaming to myself, head swinging right and left.

"Ah ha" I see on the wall a sign. "Other Platforms" to the left and "Toilets" to the right. And yes, we were slap-bang, equi-distant between the two. Looking left, I see the entrance to the tunnel at the end of the goddamn platform, some one hundred yards away. "Fuck!" that's about half an hour at Percy-speed. "Thank you, Oh Lord, thank you SO MUCH!"

Knowing the return train would be arriving any moment, we set off for the tunnel, hoping the level of imminence of the toilet need wasn't as acute as it could be. "Come on Percy, no time to waste – in both senses!" and we start shuffling along the platform.

It's no good! Even in overdrive, we are moving slower than a baby-crawl. We weren't going to make it. No choice, I'm going to have to carry him. I start twirling Percy around to find the best way to do this. Picking up and carrying a bulky and very delicate old man isn't easy, especially one who could burst at any moment. A piggyback was definitely out of the question on a toilet-ready geriatric.

I was desperate.

At this point, a man appears next to us, evidently Dutch, middle-aged, tall and balding and asks, again in very good English, if we needed help?

"Please" I replied. "We need to get to the other platform as soon as possible. The train back to Schipol goes any minute!"

The fellow suggests that together we can carry Percy, which we do. I get him under the arms and Cloggy gets Percy's legs and we start crabbing as fast as possible towards the tunnel. People were making way for us, probably assuming that it was some kind of medical emergency.

We make it to the end of the platform, turn into the connecting tunnel and get halfway through to other platform when three things occur simultaneously. I get an asthma attack; Percy's bladder let's go and our return train pulls into the station at the end of the tunnel.

We had no option but to pick up the pace. By this time, Percy was not only getting pretty bloody heavy, but is also leaking like a punctured bowser. Me and Cloggy are shuffling sideways at full throttle, I myself am completely void of oxygen, whilst Cloggy, on the wrong end of Percy is getting soaked in wee-wee. We (that's a lot of wee's) staggered out of the underpass and virtually threw Percy through the first set of open doors of the train which, thank goodness, was still stationery at the platform. I dived in after him just as the doors started to close.

"Gracias, gracias." I wheezed back to the damp Dutchman panting on the platform, his hands on his knees. What in God's name possessed me to shout "Gracias" I'll never know. Maybe my frazzled brain remembered a lot of Dutch folks go on holiday to Spain.

The train started to glide out of the station, and I managed to get Percy into a seat, now acutely aware of the smell of wee, as were some of the fellow passengers by the amount of nose-twitching going on. I fumbled in my pocket, desperately pulled out my inhaler and sucked on it for my life's worth. As I slowly managed to breathe again, we both sat silent for a while. Then, totally out of the blue, Percy says,

"When the doors shut at the airport, I almost wet myself."

We looked at each other, and the pent-up emotions erupted into hysterical laughter. To this day, it remains as one of my most precious memories shared with one of my most special people.

Arriving back at the airport, you'd think Queen Beatrice herself was on the train. Mum was waiting with a wheelchair, paramedics, a hundred and fifty rail employees, and a couple of sailors.

Percy, who was now very uncomfortable, was helped into the wheelchair, and we went up the lift into the airport. By now, check-in was just closing so we were given priority.

How embarrassing it must have been for a man of dignity, who always wears a tie, who had once fought against the Japanese in some of the most inhospitable jungles in the world, to sit, amidst other people, drenched and smelling dreadfully of urine, I'll never know. How much he himself was aware, I also will never know.

To finish, the cabin crew took pity on us and we actually had drinks in hand before take-off – Mum and I, gin and tonics, and Percy, a nice cup of tea. Bless his soul.

Footnote

Several months later, after our departure from The Netherlands, a suitcase was delivered to my brother's office in Assen. In the confusion on the train, I had forgotten my large case which was lodged between two seats. Such was the efficiency of the Dutch railway authorities, that the bag had been found and safely returned to the address on the label. Free of charge.

Nice one Cloggies!

PART II – LONG HAUL

I'm making quite a jump in time now. Prior to the long haul adventures, there were many episodes of trying to find the meaning of (my) life in the UK, occasional holiday trips to Europe, skiing trips, summers with friends and family, but it wasn't long before I was itching for much more.

I've decided to omit these short-haul experiences in favour of the more exotic adventures to distant corners of the world.

PATAGONIA

The End of the World

My first real long-haul adventure was in 1985, just after finishing university. I had a mate, Pete Simmons who had joined the oil industry a few years before and of whom I had lost track. Remember, no internet in those days, and blokes in my circle weren't very good at writing letters.

However, one day a letter did drop through my letter box, and from the stamp I could see it had come from Chile. The letter had taken almost a month to make the journey and had been forwarded on twice in the UK. I was surprised it actually found me.

It was from Pete. In the two hand-written pages he told me he had been down in Patagonia for the last six months and was on a two-year hitch (contract). He was living in an oil camp at the extreme southern tip of the South American continent, on the north shore of the Magellan strait. That's the narrow stretch of water which separates the Island of Tierra del Fuego from the main continental land mass. Apparently, it was a desolate place.

Even though Pete was no scribe, the few lines of description made the place sound awesome. Nature at it's most magnificent, no people, animals, adventure….. right-up my street!

Signing off, Pete invited me down to visit. I got out my Times Atlas of the World and poured over the relevant pages…Patagonia…. the Cordillera (Andes) mountain range, lakes, glaciers, it was beckoning me immediately. Plus, it was spring down there, autumn firmly on its way in the UK.

Most normal people would take months, if not years, to plan trip of such magnitude. I, on the other hand, decided to go, there and then. I shot round to Journey Latin America in Earls Court, specialists of the day in cheap flights to South America, and booked a direct flight to Santiago, capital of Chile, with a connecting flight the day after arrival down to Punta Arenas.

I then handed in my notice to the job of the moment and walked out. Didn't like it anyway.

Two days later, I flew British Caledonian from London to Santiago de Chile in.......Chile.

Santiago was a lively city, orderly, clean, sunny, very European in many aspects and nestled in the foothills of the snow-capped Andes. With just over one hundred kilometers from the Pacific coast to the border with Argentina up in the mountains, an hour or so by car from downtown Santiago are several world-class ski resorts. The Chileans boast that you can ski in the morning and swim in the sea in the afternoon.

I stayed overnight just outside the city centre in an up-market neighbourhood called Providencia. Even though I am not sure I can remember the name of the hotel, a Sheraton I think, I do remember it was full of Air Stewardesses. At that time Providencia was a well-to-do residential neighbourhood on the outskirts of the city centre.

I am told today that the city has extended far beyond and Providencia is now almost considered as being in the centre. Chile's economy has been doing well over the years, one of the few bright spots in South America.

After a very pleasant overnight, I made my way the next morning back to the airport for the connecting flight down to Punta Arenas with Lan Chile.

I'll mention the aviophia again. Whilst I had dreaded the trans-atlantic flight and had my usual wobblies getting on the plane in London, the whole experience of boarding the Lan Chile 737 in Santiago was, for some strange reason completely different. No nerves, no sickness. Why?

Was it that the city was just so relaxed, the airport small, clean, bright and empty compared to London? The clear blue sky, the calming view of the magnificent snow-capped Andes providing the backdrop to the airport. All calm and relaxed.

It's something I'll never know, but it's a phenomenon that continues to this day. Busy airports, large wide-bodied jets with passengers packed in like sardines terrify me. Small regional airports, smaller planes? Different story altogether.

The immaculate blue and white Lan Chile 737 was virtually empty. Direct flight, three and a half hours, flying parallel to the Andes down on our left (sorry, port) side, a direct line south to Punta Arenas, the biggest town south of the forty-sixth parallel.

We took off, I had the rear half of the plane to myself, and I gazed out of the window at the Andes on the left as the plane climbed to its cruising altitude. The sky was so blue, the snow so white, it was breathtaking.

The highest peak which I could clearly see in the distance must have been Aconcagua. Its summit remained higher than the plane until it disappeared out of sight behind us.

Security on flights in those days was different. You could even smoke on board. The stewardesses were all beautiful, at least in my eyes, always smiling, super-elegant and very friendly. All about my age, too!

As there were only about ten passengers in total on the plane, the Stewardesses were very much willing to chat, always in that lovely, accented English. I asked one of them if could visit the flight deck, again not uncommon in those days. She went forward to check with the Captain and a moment later appeared in the cockpit door and waved me to come up.

Inside the cockpit it was awesome. The sunlight was blinding, the Andes over to the left and the sky above so blue it was almost dark. To a layman like me, first time in an airliner cockpit, the number of dials, gauges and levers was mind blowing. The Captain and Copilot, both dark haired, suntanned and wearing gold rimmed RayBans educated me on what was what in perfect English. They also gave me a short tourist guide to Chile. From what they were telling me, I could spend a year here and not see everything. I must have been in the cockpit for at least an hour. I even got served a glass of champagne.

Unfortunately, such visits are now very much a thing of the past.

Right behind the flight deck were three rows of first-class seats, all empty. When I bade goodbye to the pilots, my stewardess asked me if I would like to stay there for the remainder of the trip. "......and would you like anuzzer glass of champagne, Senyor?".

It was just getting better and better. I sat there gazing down at the enormous, brilliant blue-white glaciers languishing between the rugged mountain peaks, the whole panorama sliding inexorably and silently by, seemingly not very far below.

On the left the Cordillera (pronounced Cordy- yera) and on the right the glistening blue Pacific. It was as if I was in a dream. This flight was by far one the most enjoyable and memorable commercial flights I have ever taken, and I cannot think of a flight that comes even close to having such a stunning view during the whole journey time.

Patagonia

As I had made the decision to make this trip on the spur of the moment, there hadn't been enough time for a letter to reach Pete with confirmation of my coming nor arrival details. I didn't even know his precise address. What I had done though, was talk to the office of his company in London and they gave me the telex (remember those ticker-tape machines?) and telephone number of the local office in Punta Arenas. I had then telexed them in the hope that the message would reach Pete, and someone might pick me up.

After some three hours of this heavenly flight, the plane started its descent, the Andes seeming to rise up to meet us, very quickly reaching the same height as the plane. Now I could see the sea on the left also, bright blue-green, almost transluscent, dotted with white points indicating a strong wind.

The ground started to flatten out, the wheels clunked down and we touched down in Punta Arenas. Regretfully, I said goodbye to the stewardesses, swapped phone numbers with two of them and promised to get in touch when I returned to Santiago.

An empty airport, what looked like some military planes far over the other side, and another delightfully small and empty terminal building.

And the wind!

We had to walk the hundred yards from the plane to the terminal bent over forwards to stop being blown over backwards. Even though the sun was shining brightly, the wind was fierce and damn cold. As I would find out, this wind blew three hundred and fifty days of the year down here.

Last in the line of passengers and enjoying the cold air, I entered the simple immigration hall and emerged into a small and empty arrivals hall, with little notion of what to expect.

And who should be standing there with a big grin on his face? Pete! Amazing.

After a quick beer in the terminal bar and twenty minutes of excited catch-up chat, we went out to his light-blue company Ford F-150 pick-up, complete with what looked like rocket launchers on the back.

I flung my bag in the back and climbed in the cab. At least the sun had kept it warm inside. Pete started up, the engine sounding like a Sherman tank, and we set off out of the airport, turning north to begin the two hundred and fifty kilometer drive to his base camp. Pete had thoughtfully brought a cooler box full of beers.

We kept the turquoise sea on our right, sometimes the edge only a few meters away from the road. The wind was whipping the wave crests to white. The asphalted road surface was excellent, the road dead straight and there wasn't another car in sight, either front or back. Bright blue sky, the occasional buffeting constantly reminding us of the wind outside, and a flat landscape that resembled Dartmoor with a rough stubble of brown coarse grass. Far over to our left we could see the grey outline of the Andes. This was Patagonia.

After about twenty minutes we left the shoreline and continued on through the brown undulating hills, dotted with the occasional sheep. Soon, a small sign appeared with an arrow pointing to the right "ARGENTINA".

Pete yanked on the wheel and we bounced off the asphalt and skidded sideways onto a gravel road. It was as hard as concrete and extremely rutted, like driving over a cattle grid. It was also covered in loose, sharp stones. The pick-up produced an enormous dust-cloud behind it, making a rear view impossible. Pete kept the speed up around one hundred and twenty clicks per hour and we half drove, half flew along the road, the suspension taking a hell of a beating.

When a particularly big rut came along, the back of the Pick-up would skew violently out to the side, threatening to roll us over down the bank. The first few times I nearly crapped myself, hanging onto the door handle in sheer panic. Pete didn't even notice, just expertly played the wheel bringing the Pick-up back on an even keel.

On the odd occasion a car came the other way, Pete put his had firmly on the windshield, as did the other driver. Apparently if a stone hits it, it won't shatter so easily. Neither driver slowed down, though.

Sometimes the road was cut through a hillock, sometimes it was built up higher than the surrounding grassland. You'd get ten kilometres of dead-straight track, then two or three sharp bends around the odd hillock. Pete never slowed down and the pick-up's rear-end continued its tail-end shimmying for the next two hundred kilometers.

Once we skidded sideways round a fairly tight bend to be faced with an enormous truck in the middle of the road coming right at us. On the back of the truck was a drilling rig! The massive steel structure must have been about ten to fifteen meters wide, far wider than the road itself. There was nowhere for us to pass and I yelled something un-printable and shut my eyes, waiting for impact.

Pete, not even batting an eyelid, wrenched on the wheel and we shot off the road, bounced down through the drainage ditch then shot up the side of the embankment to some fifty feet above and parallel to the road, still going at over a hundred clicks and threatening to roll-over at any moment. Out of the side window I watched the rig pass us by down below, and Pete then eased the F-150 back down onto the road.

"Pass me another beer, Mate" he grinned, obviously enjoying the moment. I didn't know at the time, but this kind of lunacy was indicative of the "living on the edge" madness of the oil patch and how it was to be for the next month. I loved it.

After another hour and a half of sliding around on the gravel roads passing through endless barren rolling brown hills, stunning blue cloudless sky and lots of sheep, we pulled into our final destination – an oil camp called Posesion (pronounced Po-zes-y-on), a settlement of oil workers five miles from the end of the world. Well, not exactly the world, but the most southern tip of the South American continent, if you don't include Tierra del Fuego. Look up Faro Punto Dungeness on Google maps – you'll see what I mean.

Posesion

Now this place was what I call remote. A collection of corrugated metal huts, containers and sheds built on a slight hillside, separated by a main drag of grey dust and white-painted stones which marked the roads. A small grass circle and a Chilean flag in front of what was the main building marked "Town Center". No trees, no bushes, some patches of barren grass, and all dusty. The sky was cloudless and blue, the wind was constantly blowing like hell, and it was cold.

Posesion was oil camp. In those days, the oil industry was pretty much a men-only domain. The local Chilean workers did a week-on, week-off from Punta Arenas, shuttling back and forth every week by bus. The very few expats like Pete worked for the international service companies. These guys did one or two months on and then had a few days leave. Thirty, sixty, ninety days continuous in a place like this! Holy shit!

We pulled up in front of a light-blue, painted hut made of corrugated steel; this was Pete's lodgings, provided by the company. Inside it was basic but warm. There were six individual bedrooms off a single corridor, a communal bathroom with two plastic shower stalls, a kitchen and a living room with a stereo and a TV. There was no TV signal as such – it was just hooked up to a VCR.

Pete walked me down to my room and gave me the low-down.

"You can use this one. It's normally Hank's room, he's a Yank, but he's offshore now. That's Keith's room, Canadian - he's on leave. And that's Pedro's room - Colombian. He's on a job but should be back tonight sometime. There's beer in the fridge, there's a bunch of videos, although the VCR is a bit shitty. We can cook and eat here, but as we haven't brought anything to cook from Punta Arenas, we'll eat in the canteen with everyone else. Welcome to the end of the world! Oh yes, we have four dirt-bikes down the shop!"

I dumped my bag, went and grabbed a beer and sorted through the videos. There were about twenty or so.

"Don't you get bored with only these?" I shouted to Pete who was having a shower.

"Don't get bored here, mate. Working all the bloody the time. 24/7!"

After a second day of relaxing, and having watched "First Blood" twice, I was starting to get itchy feet. I asked Pete if I could come down to his "shop" to have a shufty at what he does.

Next morning, we took the pick-up and drove to the other side of the camp to his operations base. Big blue hangar, inside smelling of diesel oil, with all sorts of weird and wonderful tools, hoists, winches, generators, compressors, cables, an electronics lab, a mechanics shop, an explosives bunker, a radioactive source pit, two bloody great big thirty-two ton trucks and...four motocross bikes. Whilst it was all very interesting and complex, my attention was on the dirt-bikes.

"Mine's the bigger one, the XR-250 Honda. Bloody powerful! said Pete. "Help yourself but watch it. It bites!"

So, I did. And it did, too.

Imagine this, a landscape of thousands of square kilometres of rolling hills, some small, some very high, some gentle, some steep, all covered in a rough brown grass, criss-crossed by the occasional gravel road and wire fences. No towns, to humans, nothing. The sheer sense of being "away from it all" was unbelievably exhilarating.

Five minutes in a straight-line south from the camp on the XR-250 brought me to the northern shore of the Straits of Magellan. The brown moonscape just suddenly stopped at a sheer cliff which dropped several hundred feet down to a grey shingle beach. The wind was constant, strong and cold. The sky was almost always bright blue and cloudless. The sea was transluscent turquoise, the wind whipping the crests to white. It looked stunning, but you could tell it was icy cold.

Apart from the oil camp, not a house, tree, person, car, bus, McDonalds, within two hundred miles. Just Patagonia. Brown hills and sheep. It really was spectacular.

The following days were spent happily thundering across the plains on the bike searching for Nandu (pronounced Nan-doo), small dark-black ostriches and Alpacas, the local Llamas.

I remember one time coming up close to a family of Alpacas. Beautiful animals, there was Dad, Mum and baby. Light brown in colour, the adults must have been a good six or seven feet tall. It wasn't my intention to scare them, but obviously the bike's engine had spooked them, and they bounded off across the plain until they were held up by a wire fence, about four foot high.

I followed at a distance, trying to make as little noise as possible, keeping the revs low. Anxious to get away from me, Mum and Dad both jumped the fence with ease, but the little'un couldn't. It ran back and forth along the fence, obviously scared out of it's wits, whilst the adults ran back and forth on the other side giving it encouragement. I stopped the bike and killed the engine, and just sat there resting on the handlebars, watching nature.

The adults were getting stressed by the little one on the other side of the fence. Then, one of the adults, not sure if it was Mum or Dad, leapt back over the fence and led the little one twenty yards away from the fence. It then ran forward and leapt over, encouraging the little one to follow. Again, the foal tried, but couldn't do it. Then the other adult joined in and they both jumped back and forth, showing the youngster. This went on for three or four attempts, until finally the foal plucked up the courage and took the leap, just making it over. I watched in enchanted awe as the family stopped, looked back at me as if to say goodbye, then turned and strutted off into the distance, their brown coats soon disappearing into the backdrop of the hills. Unforgettable moment.

On my daily bike rides, apart from the hundreds of thousands of sheep and occasional group of llamas, there was one other resident of the southern patagnia plains which is worth mentioning. The Nandu. A small ostrich, dark brown, about three foot high, can't fly but can run bloody fast.

I'd spend hours ripping across the terrain on the bike wearing my Walkman, (no helmet of course) listening to Billy Idol, trying to keep up with these fellows. They were so fast and agile they could change direction in an instant. An hour of keeping the bike at speed bouncing over the grassland, jumping ditches and flying off mounds trying to keep up with these birds and your whole body ached like hell.

One afternoon I got a puncture and the bike was laid up for a week or two, until someone managed to get a spare from Santiago. It's not like you could just pop down to the local Halfords for a new inner tube. It had to be ordered from Santigao, flown down, shipped out. All took time.

I often went down to the shingle beach, where there was a solitary, enormous rusty shipwreck, half buried in the beach. It was a paddle steamer, steel hulled, must have been there for at least a hundred years and was slowly rusting away, a reminder of days gone by.

Punta Arenas in it's hey-day was a very busy staging port for shipping passing through the straits to avoid going around Cape Horn. Must have been a very dangerous passage, as the current in the straits could reach eight knots, faster than one of those paddle steams would have been able to manage.

From the cliff top I could see the oil platforms out to sea, each with its own bright tongue of fire flaring off the excess gas. Small dots on the horizon, but I knew from Pete that each one had twenty or thirty men on-board, mostly Chileans and a few expats from all over the world.

Bored, in the middle of nowhere? Absolutely not.

One Sunday afternoon, again that clear blue sky and the biting wind, Pete took me down to the shop as the crew were having a barbeque. There were no jobs on, so it was a welcomed rest day. They'd caught a lamb in the morning and the foreman was in the process of gutting and skinning it as I arrived. None of the Chileans spoke any English but they were an incredibly friendly bunch, all shapes and sizes, always laughing and, as it was Sunday, were knocking back the beers and the pisco as if there was no tomorrow.

The barbeque, or asado as they called it, was a pile of burning logs on the floor, by now glowing embers, with a home-made flat iron grate eight inches above the coals. The lamb, however, wasn't to be cooked on that. The whole lamb was spread completely open and fixed to an iron cross with two horizontals which was stuck in the gound at the edge of the fire at about thirty degrees off the vertical. This allowed the lamb to be cooked slowly, slightly inclined towards the fire. It took several hours, but slow roasted over a wood fire, it was delicious. Certainly, one of the best barbeques I'd ever had.

Another source of entertainment were the helicopters. Posesion had its own helicopter base to transport the rig crews back and forth to the rigs out in the Straits. A small blue hangar, a thirty-meter square of concrete as a landing pad with a big white "H" painted in a yellow circle, and two portacabins end-to-end which served as the living quarters and offices. The pilots of the two Dauphin helicopters were all Chilean, but the two mechanics were both Brits, rotating a month on a month off. We drank beer together in the evenings, played darts, cards, anything to pass the time.

One day, one of the mechanics, Steve, told me that they would be doing a five-thousand hours test flight the following day following and asked if I'd like to sit-in on the check-flight? You kidding?

Skimming across the hills at twenty feet or dropping like a stone over the edge of the cliff, almost getting the runners wet in the sea, suddenly soaring up almost vertically to rotate at three thousand feet and plummet back towards the sea, it was awesome. I didn't realize helicopters were so aerobatic. I suspect in the highly regulated days of the modern oil industry, such antics, especially with a non-authorised passenger would be totally out of the question.

After half an hour of going completely nuts, the pilot headed out to sea and approached a rig. Talking on the radio, the pilot brought the chopper inching towards the landing deck and hovered some ten feet above it. He looked over at me and pointed at the speed indicator. It was showing one hundred knots! Later, he told me that they often land on the rigs at that wind speed.

The times when I wasn't chasing Nandu or llamas, going down a two-hundred-foot vertical cliff on a trials bike, or shitting myself in one of the helicopters, I would sit in the hut and write letters - or watch Rambo!

The Gurkha

One evening, Pete asked me if I'd fancy visiting an oil rig. I couldn't go offshore as the places were too limited, but no problem to visit a land rig.

"Sure, why not. Let's go see what you actually do" I said.

"Okay – we leave tomorrow morning, 3am!" It was now 10pm and we were sitting drinking beer.

Three in the morning – bloody hell! Four or five hours sleep at most. But that was the way it was. The oil business doesn't respect the eight-hour day. It's a twenty-four-hour business, and when the rig calls, you go.

We left the house at 3am, passed by the base to get some equipment, and set off into the hills. When we left it was dark, but by the light of the bright stars and brilliant moon, it woud have been perfectly feasible to drive without headlights.

The journey took a couple of hours of speeding and sliding over the gravel roads, no maps, but the occasional hand-painted pointer indicating the rig name stuck in the ground at every cross-roads. We'd sometime drive for twenty or thirty kilometres between signs, always becoming more anxious until the welcome indication of the next sign showed we were still on the right route.

"Don't you ever get lost?" I shouted to Pete over the roar of the engine and the thundering of the wheels over the gravel.

"Sometimes, but it's not recommended! One guy got lost last August going to a rig and nearly froze to death when he ran out of fuel. It was minus 20 degrees that night, his pick-up had stopped in an ice puddle and broke the ice, he got soaked and decided to walk. They only just found him in time!" Pete gave me a weird grin.

We arrived at the rig just as it was getting light and the morning weather had also turned for the worse.

I'll try and describe the scene. Grey and overcast, a bitterly cold wind directly from Antarctica blowing about fifty miles an hour, and we were in the middle of bloody nowhere. The rig looked like a small Blackpool Tower, all lit up.

The rig site was a hundred-meter square, levelled and cleared of brush. There were five portacabins some fifty yards off to one side, with ten or so pick-ups parked in front.

Interspersed with the howling wind was the sound of activity, high-powered diesel generators, the clanking of heavy equipment and the odd, shouted voice. This went on non-stop, rain or shine, snow or ice, 24/7.

At any one time on the rig site there would be some thirty or so local guys, each doing a twelve-hour shift. When resting, they'd be holed up in one of the portacabins. Pete told me this rig had been drilling this well for almost a year and we had been called for a shooting.

"Ehh? Who's going to shoot who?" I asked.

I had been outside the pick-up only for about ten minutes and was already feeling the icy wind cutting through my Parka, sweater and two undershirts. How the hell do these guys do this for twelve hours!

Pete's thirty-ton Logging truck had arrived an hour before we did. The local helpers had rigged up the equipment and were waiting on Pete to make the final connections. And shoot.

Another engineer, an American called Tony, was inside the truck. Tony was a trainee engineer whilst Pete was overall in charge.

Now, as I was a gringo, in the eyes of the rig crew that made me an engineer. I was also wearing camouflage trousers, so it didn't take long before I was branded 'El Gurkha'. Funnily enough, quite a few of the rig crew did actually resemble Gurkhas. Small, heavy-set, brownish skin and not entirely round eyes.

I later found out that the Gurkhas had acquired a local reputation in the Falkands war for going into battle naked and cutting off their enemies' heads. Bit exaggerated, I think, but the Chileans are not exactly on friendly terms with their Argentine neighbours.

Pete and Tony got to work in the truck, while I just watched the activity on the rig as the crew prepared for the shooting. I still didn't know what it meant!

I was standing a few feet away from the rig floor and could see a couple of guys down below in the cellar. This was a concrete pit about two meters deep below the rig floor where the wellhead was. It was filthy, lots of black mud, and most likely freezing.

A couple of the roughnecks were obviously having trouble lifting something, so I thought "Bollocks, I'll give them a hand", and with no idea what was going on, no possibility of speaking anything but English, I jumped down into the pit to lend a hand.

Half an hour later, covered head to foot in mud and crude oil, hands about to drop off with cold, but fired up from the exertions, I was getting on fine with the two fellows in the cellar. We'd manage to free the stuck valve and were locking down some manifold when I hear "What the fuck are you doing down there?" Pete was peering down at us and didn't seem particularly amused.

I just looked up, two white eyes and a big smile through the mask of mud.

"We're going to detonate in a few minutes, so get your fat arse outta there!"

Detonate what? A fifty-foot-long steel tube, 4 inches in diameter, weighing some three hundred kilos and containing two hundred explosive charges had been lowered five kilometers down into the well on a long electric armoured cable. Ten minutes later, all generators off, just the wind making a whining noise through the rig, everyone stood still and waited for the explosion far underground.

Tony's head appeared through the door of the truck. "Ready?" he shouted, I'm not too sure to whom, as all the rig crew had retired to a safe distance and it was only me and Chamo, one of the helpers standing by the truck.

Out if sight in the truck, Tony threw the safety switch and pushed the button.

Nothing.

He pushed it again.

Nada.

Tony's head appeared again. "Hear anything? Feel anything?" he asked us.

"Nope" I said, looking at Chamo who was shaking his head.

Six hours work in sub-zero temperatures and ice-cold mud, everything's all set and then what? Zip! At this point, ten extremely pissed-off rig dudes appeared out of the gloom and addressed me, the Gurkha engineer, evidently demanding to know what was wrong.

They knew this hiccup would require repeating at least a full shift of work, minimum. As for me, I made a big, cheesy grin, told them in the best Queen's English that I was a tourist, pointed to Pete and said "Ingineero" and moonwalked towards the pick-up to avoid the inevitable lynching.

We got home fifteen hours later, twenty-four hours now without sleep, exhausted, cold, hungry and ready for a hot shower. As soon as we got back, Pete was called to go on another job, so he had a quick shower and left. Without resting. So it was.

Punta Arenas

Having spent three weeks in Posesion, even with the bikes and the helicopters, even the occasional trip to a rig, I wasn't too long before I started to get bored.

Pete came back from the base one evening and said that there would be no jobs for the next two days, so how about a trip to Punta Arenas? That was the city where the flight from Santiago had landed, 250 kilometers from the base.

Nice hotel, good food, good bars and ....girls? I had packed my bag before he finished the sentence.

Apparently, there was to be a fashion show in one of the better hotels, a big occasion. When I heard about it, I was thinking "Fashion show of what? The latest overalls, deep-sea survival gear, mud-man gloves? I can't wait".

On the road, Pete drove at what must have been an average of one hundred and forty kilometers per hour with beer in hand and only the moonlight outside giving any hint of where the gravel road went.

Skidding and sliding all the way, Pete shouted that it was a women's fashion show we'd be going to. Apparently, a bunch of models had been flown down from Santiago.

I then understood why he was driving like a complete nutter. We had Tony with us in the cab, three abreast, all togged up in our smarts, the beers were flowing, and the excitement was palpable. Tony did look a bit pale though, especially the time we left the ground completely and went over a cattle grate airborne.

We eventually reached the asphalt road, drove past the airport and came into Punta Arenas. After Posesion, it was like driving into New York. Streetlights! Pavements! Shops! Restaurants! Bars! People! WOMEN!!

We pulled up in front of the Hotel Navegantes and checked in, quickly depositing our bags in our respective rooms. Then, straight down to the bar for a quick round of Gin and Tonics, then on to a restaurant for a splendid meal of Centolla (pronounced Sen-toy-ya) . This is King Crab and reputedly the biggest king crab in the world. Chile, especially the south, has the most unbelievable seafood and shellfish.

Wined and dined, we went to the fashion show in the main ballroom of the hotel. The place was packed with probably several hundred of the towns finest, and we eventually found our reserved table right at the back. Our last-minute booking meant we'd lost out to the local dignitaries and businesspeople. What we couldn't see of the show, however, we made up for with several bottles of excellent Chilean Chardonnay.

When the show came to an end, we were on fire. So now what? It was patently obvious the models might have been on Jupiter as far as any chance we'd have to meet them, and the night was still young. Tony and I looked at Pete who, with a weird grin on his face, suggested a quiet little place he knew, good atmosphere, not too expensive and where the staff were very accommodating.

We got in the pick-up (yes, I know what you're thinking - Oil workers those days didn't seem to bother too much about being over the limit) and drove the five or six blocks to this little bar, with a cute name like the Cutty Sark or something similar. Could be Jersey!

As soon as I walked in the door, I stopped dead and swallowed. If you've never been to a brothel, which I hadn't, I'm sure you'll have a mental perception. Well, this was it.

The dim red lighting was enough to make out the bar off to one side, and the rest of the space was filled with chairs, sofas, and tables. Each un-occupied table had at least one woman sitting at it, nursing a glass of something, watching the door for in-coming oil workers and sailors. Evidently the night was slow, because when we walked in, it was like payday had arrived!

Three young gringos, still reasonably smartly dressed, definitely not tourists and definitely not sailors. To the ladies, that meant only one thing. Oil workers! Meaning we had to have lots of expectation together with lots of MONEY! The girls were almost punching themselves in the scramble.

Pete confirmed to me later that we were indeed immediately pegged as what we were. Young, single and relatively rich oil workers whose money would far outlast any physical rendition. He also said we'd be much more preferred customers compared to the more frequent old, drunk, sweaty and often violent sailors. We were, apparently, a good catch.

After fighting our way through the press of large breasts, cheap perfume and "Hola mi Amor" we finally managed to sit down. I had noticed that close-up, the girls were more often than not, slightly more than just "girls". I'd put the age range from twenty-something up to fifty-something, and size range from slim to bloody obese beings squeezed into leopard-skin miniskirts and fishnets with gaping holes in them.

Within one minute, we'd been shown to a table and had three extremely expensive whiskies put in front of us. The three drinks were immediately followed by three girls, each expertly sliding uninvited onto a lap, an arm wrapping round the owner's neck. The waiter who'd brought the whiskies obviously knew the drill, as each of the girls asked for champagne, and off he trotted to get three glasses of cheap-shit fizzy white wine which would no doubt be charged as Dom Perignon.

The girl on my lap was actually quite nice – I think - and was soon trying to give me an endoscopy with her elongated tongue. I certainly didn't choose her, so how they divvied up the clients, I'll never know.

When I managed to pull the octopus off my face, I took a few moments and looked around at the other tables. It was obvious that most of the clientele had either come of a Rig or a Boat. I'd find out later that many of these fellas were coming in directly off the rigs with twelve hours and a stack of cash to kill before getting the flight home to their wives and girlfriends.

Most were a lot older than me, probably average age being aound the mid-forties. All had tattoos and most were completely pissed. None were speaking Spanish, but they didn't seem to need any translations, as there was a constant stream of wobbly bald blokes being led by a much younger girl towards a red velvet curtain and the stairs beyond. How revolting, I remember thinking. Poor girls!

By this time, my girl was getting a little impatient for a quick sally through the red curtains, a short enactment to take my money allowing her to move on to the next dude as quickly as possible.

By now, however, the previous six hours of eating and drinking was taking it's toll and I was actually more knackered than horny. Plus, I do admit the sensation of being for the first time in a real-live knocking shop where I couldn't speak a word was quite unnerving.

My Spanish, being limited to cerveza, mas cerveza and banyo (beer, more beer and toilet) I said to Pete "Tell them I'm just here for a drink, and that's all."

So, in fluent Spanish, Pete proceeds to convey my message". "Thanks" I slurred, feeling a little more secure.

At that point, three girls jumped over and started to rip off my shirt and grappled to undo my trousers. "Wooahh!" I leapt up, the girls flying through the air, along with bottles, glasses and the table. The girls, however, didn't seem ready to take "wooahh" for what it was intended, and the clawing and yelling continued, everyone laughing hysterically, especially Pete and Tony.

I managed to stagger to my feet like a bear fighting off a pack of wolves, hurl the last girl onto the next table and ran for the door, my shirt half off my back and trousers around my knees. The pick-up was right out front, so I leapt in and locked the doors.

About a minute later, Pete and Tony, in tears with laughter, came crashing out of the door pursued by about five women of different shapes and sizes, plus a very angry looking barman waving a bill in his hand. I opened the door, Pete and Tony dived in and, with half a dozen hookers banging on the doors and windows and yelling such offers as "Fuckee, Fuckee, hundred dollar! we disappeared down the street.

"What the fuck happened there?" I asked still breathless.

"I think I translated wrong" said Pete, laughing. "I told them it was your eighteenth birthday and you were there to celebrate!" He laughed even more.

It was now almost five in the morning, the only places open at this time were competition to the Cutty Sark, but even Pete said he was feeling a bit tired. Tony had passed out.

Pete started the engine, nosed slowly out of the town centre, pointed the pick-up north and drove towards the dawn's early light appearing over the horizon. There was only 250 kilometeres of dirt track back to base camp.

I took over from Pete when he started nodding off and threatening to go off the road, and I wound up driving most of the remaing hundred and fifty kilometers on a dark, frozen dirt road all the way back to Posesion. We got back around 7am as the camp was beginning to stir.

Apparently, this was a standard night out.

Oh yes, and if I remember rightly, Pete was called for a job a couple of hours later!

Offshore

Before I left Posesion, I did manage to wangle a trip onto one of the offshore rigs. The platform was probably of the same area as that of a tennis court, perched on four legs some seventy or eighty feet above the freezing Strait of Magellan.

The wind howled constantly, threatening to rip you off your feet and fling you into the sea at any moment. The whole structure was constantly groaning and swaying, lit by arc lamps shaking in the wind. There was a constant banging of heavy machinery, the roaring of the massive diesel generators and hissing of compressors, and the dark figures in hard-hats wrapped up in thermal suits working 24 hours a day. It was like something from an Armageddon movie.

The Helipad was up high, overhanging the sea, with only a small netting around the edge to stop you plummeting to a freezing death. They told me you'd last about three minutes in that water. I also remember the chopper was showing sixty kilometers an hour when it touched down. Extreme conditions to say the least, and this was late spring! I can't imagine what it must have been like in winter.

Apart from the derrick itself, the accommodation, offices, workshop and canteen were basically four containers, two on top of two. The sleeping arrangement was a series of three-high bunks with two plastic showers and a couple of toilets.

Entertainment was a three-foot circular table and a twelve-inch tube TV which just managed to pick up a grainy signal from Punta Arenas. Only one channel.

These guys spent months at a time on this claustrophobic contraption. One guy told me these rigs were babies compared to what you find in the North Sea, where the climatic conditions can be even worse. Not for me, thanks!

I only spent an hour on the rig as the chopper stopped by to pick me up on the way back. One of those "I've been there three times" moments. The first time, the only time and the last time.

Even though these guys were well paid, you wouldn't get me doing that kind of work for all the tea in China. Many years later, Pete told me that when he finally left Posesion, he'd been there for three years. In the middle of no-where.

Heading Home

Soon, the month was up, and I had to head home. Pete drove me back to the airport in Punta Arenas, and as I boarded the flight back to Santiago, I felt a curiously strong sense of leaving somewhere very familiar behind.

Strange, after such a such brief stay. Maybe it was the desolation, the simple uncluttered existence, the clear blue skies, the open spaces? Or was it the cameradie that I found from those hardy souls who worked, lived and suffered there together? Don't know.

I had just spent thirty days in the middle of nowhere, visited a couple of rigs, spent hours on a dirt bike, helped gut a sheep for a barbeque, flown in helicopters piloted by mad-men, only just avoided being torn to shreds by a crazed herd of over-weight hookers, and driven hundreds of miles around the southern coast of Chile. Oh yes, and nearly died more than once on the road..

Two things from the trip particularly blew my mind. Firstly, Patagonia itself. The stark natual beauty of how remote, expansive, clean, and un-touched it is. Secondly, the harshness of working in the oil business.

My claim to fame - I've been to the most southerly knocking shop on the planet and didn't get laid. Takes some doing - Well done Jack!

And here's a final comment. When you go and buy your petrol from Tesco's and feel like moaning at the prices, give a little thought to all the poor sods around the globe up to their necks in ice-cold mud, oil and shit. Oil companies produce and ship some eighty million barrels of the stuff every day from some of the most remote, inhospitable places imaginable, and I've just been to one.

Petrol is cheap. Trust me, I know. I'm a Gurkha!

MACHU PICCHU AND THE BOLIVAR

In all honesty, I can't remember exactly when I went to Peru, it seems such a long time ago.

I don't have any particularly outrageous moments to recount from this trip, but I'm including it as it really was a great example of pre-package tour adventure with some magnificent and memorable moments, which I hope might make your passport itch.

It was some time in the mid-late eighties. I'd flown down direct from London to Lima and booked a couple of nights downtown at the Grand Hotel Bolivar. The intention was to get used to the time-difference and also indulge myself. Even though I was on a tight budget, a little pampering is a never a bad thing, especially after a ten hour flight.

Built in the 1920's and located on the San Martin central Plaza of downtown Lima, the Bolivar was once the epitome of Lima's opulence, with an exclusive history. Today, there are much more modern offerings from the multi-national hotel chains hotel in the up-market Miraflores area. However, the Bolivar still is a place to go and see how things used to be.

Having taken a taxi through the dusty and devastatingly poor outskirts of Lima from the airport to downtown, I remember pulling up outside the gleaming white frontage and being greeted by an impeccably dressed doorman who ushered me into the cool silence of the stunning reception area. All polished wood floors, marble and ornate decoration.

After checking in, a Valet who must have been well into his eighties shuffled up next to me and insisted on carrying my bag up the long, winding staircase to my room.

During the ascent, and in between wheezes, he managed to make me understand through a mixture of a few words of English and mainly Spanish that over the last sixty years, he'd carried bags up these very stairs for Kings, Queens, Presidents, Dictators and all sorts of Celebrities.

I was thinking at this rate it was going to take another sixty to get to the top and was seriously concerned the poor old fellow might pass out. I tried to take my bag off him, but he wouldn't have it. Anyway, we eventually made it to the second floor, and he led me down the pristine corridor to my room, unlocking the door with a great big brass key on a gigantic metal fob. You don't see those anymore!

The room was airy, white curtains, white walls, polished wood floor, dark wood furniture, ornate gleaming white bathroom with an iron bath. I wondered just how many famous people had set foot in here.

I tipped the old Valet with a couple of dollars and he deferentially reverse-bowed out of the room with such a degree it was almost embarrassing to me, an un-shaven, mid-twenty something just dying to open the mini-bar. Of which, as I then discovered, there wasn't one. Room service only, but everything ordered came on a silver-tray, impeccably served.

Showered and changed, it was getting early evening, so time for a sundowner. Or more like a dust downer, as in Lima the sun never really seems to shine, and everything is covered in brown dust under permanently grey skies. Something to do with the cold ocean currents and warm land mass.

However, being inside the Bolivar gave you a completely detached feeling, like you were in another world.

Taking the stairs down to the lobby, the sound of Chopin being played on a grand piano led me to the bar just off the reception area. Large leather armchairs, lots of artworks, columns, flowers, and virtually empty apart from a what looked like a couple of businessmen and a few well-dressed tourists. You don't see those anymore either!

Some two seconds after sitting down, a very pretty and immaculately presented waitress came over and handed me an opened drinks menu, asking in lovely, accented English what she could get for me.

With just a perfunctory glance at the menu to be polite, I was about to ask for a Gin and Tonic, but instead said "What do you recommend after a long flight?", hoping to impress her with my charm.

"Has el Señor ever tried a Pisco Sour? Eet ees Peru's most famous cocktail".

"No, I never have. If it is a nice as you are, then it must be wonderful", doing my best to be debonair. "I'll have one of those".

She nodded and smiled and retreated gracefully backwards a couple of steps before turning towards the bar, knowing exactly what I would be looking at as she walked away. She would have been right.

Pisco Sours were to be drunk in copious amounts during the next week or so. Both Peru and Chile take credit for Pisco, so never say to a Chilean that Pisco is Peruvian, or vice versa!

It was actually created in the 16th century by the Spanish settlers trying to make a local version of their own home-grown liquors. Distilled from fermented grape juice, Pisco is a clear spirit, around 30-35% alcohol volume and is generally drunk as the Pisco sour – a cocktail made from Pisco, lemon juice, sugar syrup and egg white. Not a long drink, and seemingly un-offensive from a strength perspective, a Pisco Sour is very smooth, sweet easy to drink. Far too easy in fact, and in the same way as the Brazilian Caipirinha, the alcohol content is masked by the sugar, and they can creep up on the un-suspecting guzzler, as in yours truly!

I later found out that one of the Grand Hotel Bolivar's famous guests, Orson Wells, apparently drank forty-two Pisco Sours in one session! Hmm, a challenge! No doubt he was carried up the stairs by the old Valet.

Two days of opulence and timeless pampering went by very quickly, and after a good dose of sight-seeing of downtown Lima, I finally checked out of the Gran Bolivar. I hadn't got anywhere with the waitress as "el Senor eez a guest and eet not allow, but nevertheless I left Lima with fond memories to fly to Cuzco, the staging post to Machu Picchu.

Again, it was such a long time ago, I can't recall what type of aircraft it was, but it had propellers, there were chickens in cages, women in bowler-hats breast feeding babies, and, I'm sure I even remember a goat or two. Bloody kids!

Cuzco was a small, dusty town, nestling at the foot of the Andes. Back then it was quaint in a dusty sort of way, it's main claim to fame being that it is the nearest town from which to take the train to Machu Picchu.

I spent a night wandering around the tascas, listening to locals playing pan pipes usually accompanied by fellow locals strumming small guitars. These small groups of folkloric musicians could certainly kick up a lively jig, and I found myself up way beyond the intended hour enjoying the entertainment. I felt as if I was the only Gringo in town. Blame the Pisco's!

I stayed in a small hostel, very basic, but run by lovely people. Spoken English was getting rarer by the kilometer, so I was having to rely more and more on my Spanish, which had advanced from being able to ask where's the toilet and ordering a beer, to "what time is it, how much" and "can I have another Pisco Sour, please!".

Next morning, I walked the short walk to the train station for the trip to Machu Picchu. The train was an old diesel engine pulling some five or six cream and brown carriages, all pretty clapped out. No air-conditioning, half the windows were stuck open and the seating was a two-by-two configuration with the central passageway down the middle. I say passageway with reservation as it was pretty much impassable due to the amount of baggage, cages, produce and even the odd animal taking up the space.

My fellow passengers were a mixture of short, stocky, bowler-hatted local women, with their brown-leather skin and marked Andean features, lots of their offspring, and quite a few back-packing foreigners.

The train chugged along at a reasonable pace, following the grey-water river down to the left which had cut its way along the steep valley floor.

Next to me was an elderly local man in a threadbare old suit, face also like old leather, no teeth and who insisted on talking to me every five minutes. He didn't seem to mind, notice or care that I couldn't understand a word he was saying. What he did do though, was offer me a dip into his plastic bag of coca leaves.

These leaves, chewed by the peoples of the Andean nations, are a mild hallucinatory drug and are supposedly exceptionally good for you, particularly helping with altitude sickness.

Obviously, the more leaves you chew, the more hallucinatory drug you're taking on board, and I soon found out that the "very good for you" quickly turned into the "what planet am I on". As for helping with altitude, it sure gets you high pretty bloody quickly!

By the time we reached the first stop I was totally spaced-out and thirsty. I got off the train as there seemed to be no indication of it going anywhere for the next few minutes and went in search of liquid.

The water being sold in plastc bottles looked decidedly dodgy, so I opted for some tea, made with – yes, you guessed it - more Coca leaves. Thinking I might soon be in danger of overdosing on Coca leaves, I thankfully found a woman selling Coca Cola and beer. No contest!

As the train pulled out of the station I floated back to my seat and had a long conversation with the old man. I hadn't realized that Coca leaves washed down with a few beers enabled one to speak fluent Spanish with ease.

I was on top of the world and the rest of the train journey was a bit of a haze. The old diesel chugged along, all the doors and windows were now open for maximum ventilation as it was getting warmer outside in the midday sun. Most people were asleep rocking from side to side in unison. Coca again.

The river rushed along its rocky bed parallel to the tracks, whilst the valley sides towered thousands of feet above us. I tried unsuccessfully to take some photographs out of the window of the mountains, but it was difficult with the rocking of the train and the cramped space.

In normal circumstances, I would have been frustrated. However, Coca is marvellous; it just smoothes out all the problems and makes life just so serene and enjoyable. Nothing is a problem, or a worry and it was only natural that if you want to take pictures upwards and there is a roof in the way, then you simply go on top of the roof. So, I did.

I left the carriage through the inter-connecting door to the next wagon and found a metal ladder going up to the roof. I was totally oblivious to the tracks thundering past below my feet. Within a couple of seconds, I was up, sitting on the edge of the roof, feet dangling over the side, snapping away, feeling on top of the world.

I really have no idea how long I was up there. Perhaps it was the rushing wind, or St. Chris tapping on my shoulder, or the effects of the Coca diminishing, but it wasn't long before I thought I should perhaps go down.

As I got down to the last rung of the ladder and opened the carriage door, with a boom it all suddenly went dark. We had gone into a tunnel. Hmm - hadn't seen that coming. St. Christopher again?

Occasionally, the train would stop at no particular place, and people would disembark, chat for a while, have a smoke or a chew, and then hop back on. Women in traditional dress would be selling delicious grilled sweet corns and yams cooked right there on the platform.

Urchins ran around all over the place and always spotted the tourists, holding out their grubby mits in the hope of a coin.   The women wore a variety of different hats.   I was told by an obviously well-informed American lady that the hat denoted their standing in the local communities.

Would it still be like that today? I imagine you'll now have a choice of McDonalds or Starbucks, all served up by a woman from Warsaw.

Finally, after several hours, our train arrived at a medium sized station, still quaint but bloody busy. It was the end of the line, down at the bottom of the valley, with the Inca city still invisible a couple of thousand feet above us.

Outside the station was a convoy of clapped out old minibuses. Along with another twenty tourists, I produced my paper voucher and clambered aboard the first one, grabbing the front seat. The bus was so cramped a few folks had to put their bags on the roof, which were tied down with rope to a home-made roof rack which you wouldn't put too much trust in if you had the choice. They didn't.

The driver climbed in, greeted everyone with a "Goo Arternoo, we go now up Machu Picchu. Hold tie", stuffed a wad of coca leaves into his mouth and started the engine. Engaging first gear by force and with a gnashing of cogs, we lurched forward onto the dusty track which would take us to the fabled Inca City of Machu Picchu.

We pulled off, immediately turning sharply right, as the road began to rise steeply. The bus was going to struggle under this load.

As soon as we'd rounded the first bend, a young lad appeared in the middle of the road in front of the bus, waving his arms, jumping up and down, and shouting something which none of us passengers could possibly hear.

The driver didn't seem slightly interested and didn't slow. We all looked in alarm at the fast-approaching kid, and when it seemed he would surely disappear under the bus, he jumped out of the way and vanished into the dust as we trundled past.

After another fifty yards, we turned sharply left, still going up before coming to the next hairpin bend. As the driver slowed to negotiate the bend, who should pop out in front of the bus? The same boy, going through the same routine, waving madly and shouting.

Us passengers said as one "Oh look, there's that wee laddie again (not sure why I wrote that in a Scottish accent?). He must have run up those terraces as quickly as we drove the track. The kid was fast.

And this ritual continued for two thousand feet upwards, and many, many bends, the boy just beating us at every one. It was an ingenious plan, as each time he appeared he had the entire busload's attention and the applause and cheers from within increased.

Finally, some twenty minutes later we reached the summit and we all piled out, thankful to have made it alive.

And who was there to greet us? The boy, grubby face beaming like a Cheshire cat, hardly a bead of sweat on him.

We'd all been in the bus and we were all soaked with sweat. Man,did that kid make some cash! I secretly suspected he had five or six brother urchins spread down the mountain and it was all a con.

Anyway, there I was. Machu Picchu, top of the world! Blue skies, green mountains and the serene awe-inspiring sight of a thousand-year-old Inca City perched on a mountain.

Errr, no. Not quite.

That's what was on the brochure. I was actually standing in a muddy bus-park surrounded by tens of clapped out mini-buses and hundreds of tourists handing over dollar bills to the local hawkers selling green plastic dustbin liners to keep off the rain which had just started and was coming down in buckets!

The Machu Picchu ruins were no-where to be seen as the clouds were so low you could only see about ten feet in front of your face. Reminded me of the Brecon Beacons in November, only warmer.

What was unbelievable however, was the complete lack of perception of what was around me due to the clouds being so closed-in on us, blotting out everything. I could've been anywhere.

Then, all of a sudden, as if on some divine command, the clouds parted and the grey nothingness was instantaneously transformed to a brilliant colour image of bright blue sky, soaring green mountains all around and the ruins below me. It was breathtaking, the pointed green peaks above the clouds plunging down into unseen valleys below. The stonework of the ruins was just below me.

It was like being in one world, shutting your eyes and opening them to a totally different one.

Unfortunately, after only a minute or two, the clouds decided to shut off the view and the rains descended again. It stayed like that for the rest of the afternoon, whilst me and hundreds of other disappointed tourists trudged around the ruins in our green bin-liners.

Disappointed, yes, but it was the fleeting image when the clouds parted that remained with me.

As I was on a day trip, I had no option but to take the bus back down out of the clouds and the train back to

Cuzco, but I said to myself there and then that I would definitely go back.

I never did return to Machu Picchu, and maybe I will, but to you dear Reader, it's place you should go before it's too late.

JORDAN

Amman and the life of luxury

This was trip that had been on my "must do" list for a while. "Must do" list you ask? The term "Bucket list" didn't exist back then. At least I'd never heard it.

Plus, I consider the "Bucket" bit refers to what you will eventually kick when you come to the end of the line, an event I figured at that time was still a long way in the future. Provided, that is, St. Christopher continued to keep his watchful eye over me.

I had always wanted to see the Dead Sea. I'd studied it in my Geography course and the place fascinated me. The lowest part of the earth's crust not under an ocean.

So, it's off to Jordan then. And again, I'll remind you that in those days it was a different ball game to the modern-day ease of Googling "Package tour to Jordan".

Ask most folks today where or what Jordan is, and they'll most likely immediately think of Basketball or Golf.

Jordan the country is a small, landlocked state of some ten million people, once a British protectorate, and with such savoury borders as Saudi Arabia, Syria, Iraq, Palestine and Israel. I should imagine the Jordanians have spent a great deal of their history doing their best to not piss off the neighbours!

Anyway, not one to lash out hard-earned cash on hotels and tour guides, my trips were nearly always organised at the drop of a hat with minimal or no planning. I just winged it and took things one day at a time.

However, on this occasion, I had been given a contact by my Mother, who was at that time a private tutor in Hampshire. She knew someone who was working as a Governess in Amman, Jordan's capital, tutoring the son of.......? I won't say who, at her request, but the fellow was a bigwig in Jordanian politics, and his son needed special educational help.

Many years later, before I even wrote this book, I read in the papers that after playing a big behind-the-scenes role in post-war Iraq, the man had recently died.

Anyway, back to the story. I had planned to spend only a week in the country and arrived in Amman via Cairo. I can't remember the airline, but I do remember it was absolute crap.

Oh yes, and it was Christmas week, 1985.

First challenge on arrival was to survive the immigration procedures of the International airport which resembled a souk with the volume turned up.

Seemed like everyone was arguing with each other all the time. I passed quickly enough through customs, where the few officials who weren't elbow deep in unfortunate travellers' open suitcases looking for bribe potential, had shown a distinct lack of interest in me, A tourist who had no suitcase meant nothing to confiscate.

I eventually popped out into the arrivals hall and yet another theatre of mayhem. However, to my relief, I immediately spotted my name on a card held by a small, brown-skinned man with a black moustache. Shifty black eyes and wearing a slightly shabby, black suit, he looked the stereotype Middle Eastern driver.

"Mister Jack! I Mounir! Welcome. Welcome. Please sir, where you bag?" miming vigorously as if carrying a heavy suitcase.

"Hello Mounir. No bags. Let's go". I replied, indicating my shoulder bag. I always travel light.

"Hokay Hokay! Come, please!" He turned, screwing the paper sign into his pocket as I followed him out of the bedlam of the terminal building. Right out front was a gleaming, black Mercedes, parked in line with other vehicles of the rich, privileged and Diplomats.

Mistakenly expecting a blast of warm air, it was out into the cold and rain. Not being able to Google "Average temperature in Amman" in those days, I admit I had assumed "Middle East" meant hot, but it certainly wasn't that day. Even parts of the Middle East can get bitterly cold in winter.

So, for about an hour, Mounir elbowed the Mercedes through the maelstrom of Amman traffic, reasonably well organized in terms of roads, but extremely disorganized in terms of drivers. I suspected the highway code was limited to instruction for camels and the herding of goats.

Eventually, we glided into what was obviously the rich part of town, as everything became much calmer, fewer cars, wider tree-lined avenues, large mansions and altogether much more sedate in every aspect. Even the sun came out. I reckon it wasn't so much of "the sun shines on the righteous" as "the sun shines on the wealthy".

We pulled up in front of two enormous black wrought iron gates, with an armed guard on either side. The gates immediately swung open and we purred though, up a manicured driveway to park outside the enormous house.

Much to Mounir's disappointment as he skidded round the back of the car, I opened the car door myself, and stepped out. I immediately came face to face with a well-to-do, grey-haired lady who introduced herself with a warm, genuine smile. "Welcome – I am Geraldine. Lovely to meet you. I have been looking forward to you coming." Mother's friend.

I held out my hand feeling slightly ashamed of my two-day un-shaven stubble and back-packer appearance as she said "Did you have a good flight. I hope Mounir took care of you. You will probably want to get cleaned up". I suspect it might have been slightly more than a polite enquiry.

"Let me show you to your room. Then, afterwards, I'll introduce you to the…er… family."

The word "family" was said with a strange emphasis.

"Come. Mounir will bring your bags". She had obviously assumed the bag hanging off my shoulder was cabin-baggage and my Louis Vuitton trunk was still in the car.

I followed her through a series of spotless halls, corridors and stairways, all in beige marble and which gave me the distinct impression of what it must be like inside a Mosque. Silence prevailed.

I could write quite a bit on the "family", but I won't as it's not the point of the story, nor am I one to comment on other people's family idiosyncrasies. I'll just say it was an upper-class, wealthy Arabic family, governed by a Master of the House who I never saw or met, a wife - there was only one as far as I knew - a couple of teenaged daughters and the son.

What was immediately apparent was that the Master was exactly that. Everyone and everything lived below his mantra and order, Geraldine included. No family evenings in front of the TV eating pizza watching JGT (guess) here!

Looking back, learning how they were, the family dynamics, the imposed discipline, the two spoiled sisters straight out of Cinderella, it was not a place for me.

It was so completely alien to me as a Westerner. Plus being an alcohol-free household as are most Muslim homes, I immediately discounted the chance of a Christmas glass of port being left out for Santa Claus coming down the air-conditioning flue.

Anyway, the long and the short of it was that I was only going to be there for a few days, so I would probably survive without going completely mad. In conspiratorial conversations with Geraldine in "our quarters" in the evenings, it was apparent she wanted out as soon as possible and was counting the days to the end of her contract.

The Dead Sea

So, let's move on quickly to the main points of the Jordan trip.

The first expedition was with two of the children down to the Dead Sea. Mounir turned out to be an agreeable fellow, but please don't confuse agreeable with "would I trust him". This was the Middle East, where sons plot against each other, sons plot together against their fathers, fathers plot against their brothers and cousins, families plot against other families, clans plot against clans and they all hate the Infidel. Well, that's what Leon Uris said, anyway.

Mounir, now driving a big Range-Rover, scored highly on the agreeability-ometer that day because shortly into the journey, he pulled up outside a dodgy looking grocery store, disappeared inside and came out with a bag of Coca Cola's and sweets for the Kids, water for Geraldine and two six-packs of cold beers! I couldn't believe it.

He closed the door, and with me in the front passenger seat, we drove off, with myself and Mounir happily tucking into the beers. Yes, him driving, and yes, him a Muslim.

Thinking back on it, Mounir could probably have done whatever the hell he liked, as the influence of his employer would always provide a "get-out-of-jail-free" card and anyone driving a big black Mercedes or a

Range-Rover in Amman was obviously an un-touchable.

He also seemed to be very streetwise and he looked after his charges with a high degree of responsibility.

The drive from Amman to the Dead Sea is one great big hill downwards. It's only about 20 miles or so, but with the traffic it seemed much further.

Interesting to note that whilst Amman is between two and three thousand feet above sea level, the Dead Sea's surface is some fourteen hundred feet below sea level. The bottom of the Dead Sea is another thousand feet down, making it the lowest place on the planet that is not below an ocean. Due to it's extremely high salt and mineral content, the Dead Sea is completely void of any marine life. It is famous for its buoyancy and beneficial properties of the mud along the banks.

When you get to the shore you are filled with a sense of awe, a sense of eeriness, a sense of…time was? No waves, just a simmering silver-blue sheen. It looked like mercury.

Mounir parked up as close to the water as possible and the kids then excitedly donned their swimsuits and ran down to the edge, completely ignoring Geraldine's shouted instructions.

Mounir and I followed behind, bringing what was left of the quickly warming beers. I could see Geraldine was not at all relaxed as she had the overall responsibility of the brats.

The level of the Dead sea is steadily falling due to evaporation; hence the shoreline is slowly receding leaving a variety of stepped rocky ledges, salt pools and marshes. At the time of my visit, there were lots of small, spa-type resorts which were pretty run down and had obviously been at the water's edge when they were built.

As the water's edge was getting further and further from the main road over time, these sad, run-down buildings were now quite a way from the water, isolated in the muddy banks. It required a short walk from the main road down to the water's edge. Lots of mud, lots of crusty salt and pretty smelly.

Cashing in on the Dead Sea's tourism potential, today there are now a multitude of modern mega-hotels built with their own false beaches, all-inclusive packages, swimming pools and swim-up bars. Another example of mass tourism spreading its ugly tentacles.

All I had really wanted to do was see the Dead Sea. Just to look at it. I knew it was basically a big bucket of very salty water full of minerals. Having recently been in the turquoise, transparent paradise of the Maldives, I hadn't really intended on going for a swim. Maybe it was the beers, maybe it was being out in the open, but I thought "Bugger it, why not?" and decided to see if it was true that you really can float on your back and read the paper?

I pulled off my clothes down to my skiddies, which I assured Geraldine were surfing shorts, but which were, in fact long boxers, and picked my way down to the water's edge.

I gingerly entered the water, picking up speed through the shallows and then diving in head-first as I normally do. Arms outstretched, I glided underwater, feeling the warm, cleansing sensation of the brine, energizing after the journey in the Range Rover.

I surfaced, or rather popped out like a cork due to the buoyancy effect applying around twenty kilos of upthrust and, forgetting this wasn't the same as the Indian Ocean, struck out in a fast crawl. And then I made a huge mistake - I opened my eyes!

Now this is why I will never forget the Dead Sea. Not for its eeriness, nor its buoyancy effect, but because, unless you have a burning desire to lose your sight, you should not, under any circumstance, get any of that water into your eyes.

After two strokes, it felt as if someone had stuck two kebab forks into my eyes. Straight out of the fire. The pain was so excruciating that my eyes automatically clamped themselves shut. I tried opening them, but my body's reflex defense mechanism was having none of it.

I stopped swimming and immediately started treading water, flailing my arms and legs in the normal "I'm drowning!" fashion. This was, however, completely un-necessary due to the buoyancy. If my eyes had not been clamped shut and I hadn't been in panic mode, I would have realised I could have basically sat down floating. I had lost all sense of direction, was completely blind and had no idea which way was the shore.

From the shore, Mounir was watching all this and probably thinking I was being eaten by a shark, ignorant to the fact there weren't even fish.

Geraldine was now desperately trying to get the kids to come out of the shallows as she didn't know what was going on and had probably seen Jaws. The kids, however, were oblivious to anything and everyone.

After what seemed like several minutes, still in agony and eyes locked shut like a new-born baby, I managed to make contact with the bottom which was a feat in itself as the bloody water wouldn't let me sink. I then did what any self-respecting punk rocker would do and pogo'ed to the shallows, groaning with agony.

God knows what the folks on the shore were thinking, as there were now quite a few onlookers hoping for drama and tragedy. By now the kids had noticed and the effect on them was quite dramatic. Thinking I was being eaten alive they shot out of the water pretty bloody quickly.

I dragged myself out of the shallows and staggered up the beach arms outstretched like a Mummy. "Towel! Water!"

After twenty minutes of towel dabbing, rinsing my eyes with bottled water and a few more tots of beer, I was eventually able to keep my peepers open for more than a few seconds but with eyeballs so red even Dracula would have been proud.

With all the excitement, both Geraldine and Mounir were now ready to go home, the kids seemingly having lost their appetite for the water.

Yours truly, however, was not about to be beaten by a few grams of sodium chloride and was intent on having another go.

This time far more cautiously, making sure all orifices above the nipple line were well out of water's reach, and taking a magazine and one of the last remaining beers, I gingerly crept through the shallows and let the water exert its magic.

I could now appreciate the amazing effect of the buoyancy, being able to fully sit up as if in a deck chair. I could read my magazine, all four limbs totally in the air, the pages kept dry as a bone. It was awesome and an experience not to be forgotten. In fact, two experiences not to be forgotten.

I'd recommend a visit to the Dead Sea while you can before it gets over-crowded with big hotels, or it dries up. Or worse still, one or more of Jordan's neighbours decides to upset the status quo, which in that part of the world is an ever-present possibility.

The King's Highway

The second trip of note whilst in Jordan was a drive from Amman to El Aqaba, a port city on the Red Sea coast, and Jordan's only outlet to the sea.

Pronounced "El-Ak-a-buh", it was made famous to the western world in recent times by the movie Lawrence of Arabia, when the Arab forces defeated the Ottoman defenders during the First World War.

If you look up El Aqaba on Google, you'll see the place has a fascinating history and is crucial to Jordan's economy for trade as well as tourism. The incredible Yamanieh coral reef just offshore makes it one of the best dive sites in the world.

On this particular drive, there was no Mounir. I had rented a shitty old Toyota Corolla and convinced Geraldine that a bit of freedom was necessary. I suspect, even though she was twice my age, and not particularly impressed by the look of the Toyota, she was keen on a bit of adventure and certainly welcomed the chance to escape the disciplined confines of her employer.

The Toyota was far from new, the AC barely worked, and the radio-cassette (remember those?) sounded dreadful. But that didn't matter. I was free and doing what I like best. Driving in strange and exciting parts of the world.

With Geraldine navigating, we headed south out of Amman on the famous King's Highway towards Petra.

I'll mention here that I sorely regret not having pulled off the road and visited this ancient city, but it was actually Geraldine who told me that you don't just "pull off the road" to visit Petra – you really need several days to appreciate the incredible stone-carved architecture. I'll just have to include it in my Bucket List!

Besides, I was having way too much fun on the King's Highway.

Imagine the M25, somewhere around the M3 interchange, five lanes each way including the hard shoulders. Now, take away every single barrier, including the central dividing Armco, remove all signposts, erase all white lines, forget any speed cameras, and you are basically left with a bloody great swath of black tarmac runway about one hundred and fifty feet wide. Now add to this lots of winding hills, a highway code designed for   camel trains and goat herders. No apparent rules for motorized vehicles apart from "take no prisoners!" and, to cap it all, there was me, a driver with several years hardened experience with a West London Courier company.

Poor Geraldine had really not seen this coming at all.

After only a few kilometres out of the city, it was immediately obvious to me that it was far more dangerous to go slowly and drive carefully. It was also evident that absolutely every motorised vehicle, whatever the size, age, load or mechanical condition, was going at it's maximum speed.

So, there we were, bombing along at maybe eighty miles an hour, weaving through the vehicles on any side you fancy. You could see the drivers' faces as you passed, totally affronted by being overtaken and doing everything they could to catch you up and retake the lead.

Geraldine, God bless her, spent most of the time with white knuckles clutching the seat belt and not saying very much.

Soon the highway started to climb, weaving its way around the hillside contours. Now there was more of a segregation of the slower trucks and the faster cars, but it was still a racetrack.

Suddenly, coming around a fairly tight bend with tyres squealing on the smooth tarmac surface, we were confronted by six petrol tankers in line abreast, taking pretty much the whole width of the highway. Three were coming down towards us and three were climbing in the same direction as us, all belching black smoke. The slowest was going up at less than walking speed, and the fastest coming down, smoke coming from it's over-heating brakes, was probably going only slightly faster. It was simply a blocked road!

Like a darting pilot fish around a whale, various small vehicles coming down from the opposite direction were going far too fast to stop and were most likely completely out of control. Cars were zipping through gaps or going around the sides, overtaking wherever they thought the quickest route was through the mayhem.

In an instant I had to decide whether to hit the brakes and get demolished from the rear or just go for it. Fast Courier instincts took over and I went for it. I spotted a gap opening up between two of the oncoming trucks on the other side of the road, which seemed to be about half the width or the car. I lined up and basically shut my eyes. Geraldine's had been shut for quite a while.

Even though the Middle East is steeped in religion and religious history and Islam was certainly the local favourite, I reckon St. Christopher must have been in the area, because this was one of the times that he certainly took care of things! Two seconds later we emerged unscathed on the other side of the truck-wall, both wing-mirrors of the Toyota snapped back presumably from the mudflaps of the trucks on either side.

I was shrieking like a Banshee. Geraldine, on the other hand, long since having given up on the polite admonishments of "Don't you think we had better slow down" let out a stream of invective I didn't expect her to know, let alone use.

Shrieking with fear she performed an acrobatic miracle for someone of her age and virtually backflipped into the back seat. Had she also worked at Fast Courier?

Having survived that incident and knowing I was invincible, this continued for most of the day, occasionally joining in a communal race between crazy Jordanians, who had the advantage of knowing the road well. I held my own and my nerve as it is a well-known fact that the two fastest vehicles in the world are the Builders' Transit and the Courier's van.

Every so often, we'd pass a burnt-out truck on the side of the road. The already parched earth was further blackened, and the tarmac had melted, not only around the lorries' burnt-out carcasses but had run down the gullies where the burning fuel had flowed. I was convinced that some of these juggernauts most likely still had dead drivers behind the wheel.

Geraldine was unusually quite for the rest of the journey. Well, she had wanted some adventure, no?

We finally reached El Aqaba, found a place to eat on the coast and I went windsurfing. We stayed in a small hotel we had previously booked, took in some of the waterfront sights and returned the following afternoon, this time at a more sedate pace as Geraldine seemed to have aged a few years and pleaded for mercy.

Back in Amman, the remaining few days passed far too slowly as the desire to be off on adventure was still alight. Unfortunately, I couldn't change my air ticket without a severe penalty which I couldn't afford, so Petra would have to wait. I said my goodbyes to Geraldine, a quick nod of thanks to the indifferent glances of the host family and Mounir took me to the airport where we bid each other a friendly goodbye.

I boarded the plane without incident, happy to leave the mayhem of Amman and headed to London with an overnight stop in Cairo.

The Giza Pyramids

Cairo. Now there's a place.

It had never been on my list of places to go. Dirty, smelly, hot, over-crowded, everyone trying to rip you off, friend or foe and with a virtual certainty of getting the shits. No thanks. I like open spaces and nature.

But then there were the Pyramids. Hmmm....a must see.

After the particularly cramped and smelly two-hour flight from Amman, I over-nighted in a hotel in the airport terminal building.

In the times before inner-wall insulation and sound-proofed windows, the architect had obviously thought the bedroom windows should directly overlook the runway for a nice view of the aeroplanes.

With the advent of the jet engine, however, a good night's sleep became completely out of the question unless, that is, you do actually sleep better when the room physically moves every two minutes with the sound of Krakatoa erupting, threatening to explode the window glass. Dreadful.

After a good night's sweat and tremble and virtually no sleep, I had most of the following day to spare before the flight to back to London. Enough time for the Pyramids!

Looking at the hundreds of crappy tourist flyers in the room, as time was tight I decided to use one the local tour companies.

I will take a moment to remind you that an organized tour for me was absolute anathema. I don't do such things. However, in the little time I had, and in the knowledge that I probably wouldn't be setting foot in this shi.... sorry, Cairo ..... again, I'd go for it. Plus, it seemed cheap.

Downstairs, I headed for the tourist information desk where I had been instructed to present myself at 10am. The lobby was mayhem, as mayhem seemed to be order of the day everywhere in the Middle East. Unless of course, you were rich, in which case it is a world of black Mercedes' and silent, incense and pampered luxury. This hotel reception area was like all public buildings. Mayhem, over-crowded and with the unique smell, something between coffee, joss-sticks and un-cleaned toilets.

The lobby was filled with hundreds of aircrew, tourists, hotel staff, folks in suits, folks in blankets, bags and trolleys. As usual, everyone seemed to be arguing with everyone else in as loud a voice as possible. Standard stuff.

It was now approaching half past ten and I was beginning to get pissed off. "Where's the bloody tour rep?"

Suddenly, a fellow tapped my shoulder and said "Pyramid tour? Mini-bus come now, sir". He looked like a cross between Tommy Cooper (with the fez) and Mounir.

"I've been waiting twenty minutes and am in a hurry. You said it leaves at ten. It's twenty-past already!" I shot back, already having regretting having made the decision to go.

"Tour need minimum four people, sir."

"Where are the others, then?" I demanded, fully conscious of the deficit of three.

"They come soon. No worry".

"No worry, my arse." I thought. It was plain to me there were no additional three punters, but the bloody tour wasn't going anywhere with just me. And I had already paid.

Realising that if we didn't go soon, I would be in danger of missing my onward flight. I decided I had two choices. Offer to pay for the other three, which wasn't going to happen or be creative.

I grabbed a handful of flyers from the information desk and spent the next ten minutes walking around the lobby and out into the terminal building shouting in my best Queen's English "Pyramid tours, leaving in ten minutes. Very good price. Perfect for transit passengers with not much time! See the pyramids before your flight. English speaking guide!"

Within five minutes, I had my three punters. Maybe I looked trustworthy in the very untrustworthy Cairo airport environment. I swear the tour fellow was ready to offer me a job there and then!

Positively grinning, the guide shepherded us outside the terminal to the awaiting mini-bus and off we went, heading south of the city. If I had received a quid for all the hot places I've been to in the world, where you get into a boiling, smelly vehicle and the driver starts the engine and makes a big show of switching on the AC which you know doesn't work, I'd be a rich man. This minibus was an example of such.

As it turned out, the tour was bloody great. Or at least the first bit. The minibus sweated and bumped us through an hour or so of outer Cairo suburbs and slums with nothing really pleasant about the ride, but with the excitement mounting as the sightings of Pyramids became more frequent and more and more impressive. We eventually got to Giza and piled out, much closer to the base of the Pyramids than I had expected.

They were spectacular. Unbelievable. Until you've been to see them, up close, you have no idea how awesome the pyramids of Giza realy are. Put them on your Bucket list, dear reader!

Anyway, out of the van, I completely ignored the tour guide who was doing his best to manoeuver the other three into a group for guiding and who were, in turn, completely ignoring him, busy taking pictures.

I ran straight for the base of the Great Pyramid, the biggest of the three, with only one intention. To climb it. Amazing, no fence, no guards' rails. Just the first row of massive stones.

The blocks were astonishingly huge, making the going very difficult. After twenty minutes or so, I was halfway up, when I caught the frantic calling of the excited tour guide wafting up on the warm wind. I looked down and could see him gesticulating, far below. It was obvious the bus was leaving.

Fuck, fuck, fuck! Climbing this Pyramid had suddenly become life's priority, and it wasn't going to happen, unless I lost my ride back and lost my flight. An immediate decision had to be made! Eyes rolling, finances and reason prevailed and, annoyed beyond belief, I jumped my way back down and got on the bus.

To rub salt into the wounds (as if, after The Dead Sea, I needed more), the reason the bus was leaving so soon was to go directly to the guide's brother's gift shop which was full of absolute crap, followed by his cousins' coffee shop, prior to arriving at his friends' camel ride venture.

The only reason the guide and the driver were not killed on the spot was that I had heard about Egyptian jails.

I was livid then, and my blood boils even today when I think back. There I was, halfway up the Great Pyramid, and the one and only time I took a bloody guided-tour and it all went to shit. Because I was on a tour.

145

And that was that, back to the airport, and back to Britain.

Today, it is forbidden to climb the Pyramids.

THE MORROCAN WEDDING

Talking of stings, such as in the Cairo Pyramid tour, there was not too much drama to this trip, which was another spur-of-the-moment adventure, but did include another a lesson in life.

I never had much inkling to travel to any of the North African countries. Lots of sand, lots of extremism, no alcohol and a very good chance of being beheaded. Plus, a lot of French is spoken.

However, a friend of mine, Pete who you'll remember from a previous chapter and who had gone abroad to work in the oil fields in South America, had been invited to go to the wedding of a colleague in Casablanca, Morocco. You know..."Play it again Sam", and all that? I always liked that movie.

The guy who was to get married was an American, bloke called Chris Sheehan. Apparently, he'd been on vacation in Spain where he met a Moroccan girl, Roya, who was studying in Valencia. Turns out she was some fifteen years Chris' junior, totally exotic and bewitching and he had immediately fallen head-over-heels and announced within the space of two months that they would be married.

In Morocco.

As you do!

I heard that in the month after the decision was made to tie the knot, Chris had visited Morocco to meet the family, had been given the head-man's blessing and all was good.

The wedding was to be held in Casablanca where Roya and her large family (would that be a tribe?) lived.

It was going to be the Full Moroccan Monty, a traditional marriage, hundreds of guests from the bride's side, one or two of Chris's lot, with all the bells and whistles and of course, bouzoukis.

That's pronounced "bazooky" to the common man, a stringed instrument favoured by Mediterranean's north, and to me can be likened to Flamenco, or sailing. Good for the first five minutes then you want to kill someone!

Anyway, Chris had invited Pete who in turn invited me. Seems like Chris was in need of western back-up, so there was I, invited to Casablanca for the wedding of a bloke I had never met. Still, Casablanca did sound exotic, Pete said it would be fun, so I booked the ticket.

I had arranged to go out from London on the same flight as Pete, and as it was only a three-hour flight on a relatively small plane.

The two of us arrived in Casablanca airport and it took less than ten seconds to realize that the Casablanca of Humphrey Bogart was long gone or probably didn't even exist at all. Mayhem in the airport, mayhem outside the airport and mayhem on the way to the hotel.

The taxi looked like it would fall apart any moment, smelt inside of what I can imagine a camel shed would smell like, and the constant bedlam of Moroccan music screeching out of the crappy radio was only drowned out by the driver blowing the car horn every five seconds.

After a tense thirty-minute rally we baled out at the hotel, brushed off the dust, and entered the cool, calm marbled serenity of the lobby. Money here, I thought. A shout came from our left and there was Chris on a stool in the lobby bar, obviously enormously relieved to see a familiar face. Pete's, not mine. Chris was a tall fellow, looked like a living skeleton, but was very friendly and courteous.

As the ceremony wasn't until the following day, we relaxed and had a few beers. Chris told us there were going to be nearly two hundred guests, four of which were westerners and three of them were at present sitting at the bar. Bob, the remaining 25% of the blue team would arrive that night from Atlanta. The wedding was to be an all-day affair going on to the early hours, lots of dancing and, oh..errr....sorry, no booze! It's a Muslim wedding.

"You what??" came out of me and Pete in perfect stereo.

"Hold on, hold on" said Chris quickly, "we have a small room set aside for the non-muslims only. In there, we'll put a secret stash. Only for us". Pete and I both sat down, and the smiles returned to our faces.

It transpired that all this shebang in one of the best hotels in Casablanca was to be paid for one hundred percent by Chris. His immediate family apparently didn't have any money and weren't coming. Nor were any of his relatives.

We sensed that the marriage was probably not approved of back in Chicago. Also, we didn't ask what the custom in Morocco was about paying for a wedding, but a few small bells were beginning to tinkle.

After an hour or two's chin wagging, Chris had to retire to do some organizing, which probably meant paying for something or other. He left.

That left Pete and I at a loose end for the rest of the day before Bob would arrive later that evening. So, what to do in sunny Casablanca?

The Anfa Royal Golf Club

We asked at Reception for tourism options and were told about the stunning Mosque, the market, the Corniche and the small golf course within the horse racing circuit, right in the center of the city...."Whoa, Whoa" we said. "Golf in downtown Casablanca?" That has to be seen!

We downed our beers and jumped into a cab which took us to the Anfa Royal Golf Club. Yes, it was set in the heart of residential Casablanca at the Anfa-Casablanca racecourse, and had been there since 1942. Must have been around Humphrey's time as there were signs of the old colonial splendor, but much face-lifting was needed.

We hired two bags of motley clubs and with the sun blazing, we marched enthusiastically across the sandy home stretch of the racetrack to the first tee, which we expected to be empty.

It wasn't.

There was an enormously overweight bloke going about the motions of teeing off. Seeing us walk up, as much of a surprise on his face as on ours, he introduced himself, in a deep, southern-state American accent, as Brad, and asked if we would like to join him?

Absolutely, and we shook hands. I then asked him - and I'll always remember this - if he had a handicap.

He replied "Yeah..aaa gat two. Bad breath and a small dick!" This was going be fun.

The bets were placed, deciding on bingo, bango, bongo format. Don't worry, I won't go into it.

Anyway, the golf course was, in terms of quality, pretty crappy, the quality of golf played was pretty mediocre, but Brad was a laugh, and the fact that it was in the middle of a colonial racecourse in the middle of Casablanca made it a very memorable and enjoyable few hours.

A few beers in the bar with ceiling fans afterwards saw Brad depart, and both Pete and I were convinced he'd be going back to his CIA desk.

To cut this short, we eventually got back to the hotel, got showered, and went down to the bar to meet Bob, who looked like he'd just flown thirteen hours from Atlanta in Economy. Which he had.

Suitably refreshed, we headed out for a Moroccan dinner to a restaurant highly recommended by the hotel, no doubt the Concierge's brother's place, and with low expectations, continued on afterwards to a night-club.

What a surprise! It was evident that the young (rich) Moroccan partygoers were the same as young (rich) partygoers anywhere in the world and a good time was had by all.

Unfortunately, even though we tried, we couldn't get the girls back to the hotel as that would have been far too riskée for them, so that was that and drunken and effusive farewells were slobbered on the hotel's steps as they drove off, music full blast, laughing and shrieking as only young, rich carefree folks do.

The Big Day

The big day dawned. It was awesome. We convened at around 4pm, but it was obvious that a lot had been going already during the earlier part of the day. The main room was enormous, about fifty tables, lots of flowers and a mixture of guests from the young and fashionable in high-dollar outfits, to the old and distinctly un-fashionable, poorly dressed and smelling of sheep. A complete cross-section of Moroccan society. I also distincty remember the lights. It was very, very bright. All the time.

The majority of the men were in suits, most of them shiny and tightly buttoned, whilst the younger women wore well-fitting, brilliantly coloured, long dresses. There were some absolute stunners. There were also a lot of old folks, generally sitting as couples, the men in shabby suits and the women looking decidely unfriendly. And then there were the kids, generally well dressed, millions of the little buggers, constantly running around and shrieking.

Hundreds of people, the biggest banquet I've ever seen, and more bouzouki music than at a bouzouki convention. Non-stop noise.

After some three hours of the bright lights, the bedlam, and lots of dubious-looking food, the expectancy level rose, the end doors opened, and the bride was carried in. In true Cleopatra style atop a beautifully ornate sedan chair carried by four guys, each looking like Sinbad.

Chris, dressed up like a tall Aladdin in a short carpet-sellers clothes, shuffled along behind, giving the distinct impression from the sickly smile on his face that he had just received the bill.

The feast went on for bloody hours, with all my favourites. Cuscous, yuk, rice, yuk, goat's "bits", sheeps eyeballs, yuk, all washed down with lashings of yummy ginger beer, and oddly tasting milk. There was some vaguely recognisable lamb stew, though, thank God.

Pete, Bob and I secretly enjoyed our private stash, every now and then disappearing to go and 'freshen up' and have a good old swig of Johnnie Walker in the linen cupboard.

After the meal, the dancing began in earnest. In fact, no, that's not true. The dancing had started in earnest in the mid-afternoon. The Moroccans, young, old, male, female, whatever, seemed to like dancing. Individually, in pairs, in groups, you name it. No inhibitions whatsoever.

Plus, they didn't need a dance floor, but right there between the tables. Blokes danced with blokes. Girls with girls. Only established couples seemed to dance bloke and girl. They were unbelievably extrovert. In western eyes they often looked bloody ridiculous, but they enjoyed themselves enormously.

Just imagine it, three western blokes in ill-fitting suits and ties, sitting at a table covered in inedible food, glasses of milk, unable to clutch the comforting pint so essential to any nocturnal activity in their world, listening to blaring bazouki music, watching these Moroccans having a blast.

There was one moment I'll never forget. Two Moroccan fellows, middle aged, bright faced, flushed with happiness and maybe too much goat's milk, got up and started dancing together, a mixture of Zorba the Greek and Belly dancing.

They soon found themselves girating in front of our table, and probably unaware of our total discomfort they started making all sorts of provocative moves towards us. The rest of the room was clapping. Then, one of them grabs Bob by the hand to pull him up. The look of sheer, unadulterated horror on Bob's face was a sight to behold. You don't do that sort of thing in Hicksville, Tennessee. He wiggled and pleaded until his genes got the best of him and I thought he was going to floor the two of them there and then. Me and Pete were crying laughing.

To save the moment, the two Moroccan fellows were suddenly replaced by the most beautiful exotic girl, who straight away changed Bob's demeanour for the better, but before he could make anything of it, was immediately replaced by a fat old bag and her husband, the music now getting louder by the minute.

And all in the brightest of lights and no place to hide. Incredible.

The frequency of the visits to the secret stash increased, allowing good old Johnny Walker to remove the inhibitions that us westerners so badly suffered from and the Moroccans didn't, and we were soon up and bazooki-ing with the best of them. A good time was had by all and even though I can't remember what time it all ended; the sun was most definitely coming up.

Next day both Pete, Bob and I had to leave early to the airport but had enough time to make a quick trip to the Hassan II Mosque on the water's edge.

Built over seven years and finished in 1993, it is absolutely spellbinding. One of the most impressive and awe-inspiring buildings I have seen to date. Going inside you are transported from the dusty heat of the city to a silent, cool, serene world of dark wood, insense and marble.

In awe of the Mosque and hung-over from the whisky the night before, we got a taxi back to the hotel and said our goodbyes. Lots of smiles and hugs and kisses from the few guests that were up and around at that time to see us off, even if none of us understood a bloody word the other one was saying.

I found out later that in a Moroccan wedding the bride and all her entourage (ie best friends) need to change clothes seven times throughout the proceedings. So, Chris' missus had about ten close friends so that's …what…seventy dresses to be made and paid for?

Then there was the ceremony. And the hotel. And the bouzoukis. Poor Chris.

Footnote

About three months later, I got a call from Pete. A couple of months after the wedding, Chris' new mother in-law suddenly needed a hip replacement. He'd also bought a house in Casablanca for them when they were "in town".

A month after that, his wife vanished into thin air. Before she did, and I don't know all the in's and out's of how she managed it, but she had got Chris to sign over the house to one of her associates, plus a substantial amount of money.

Seems like the whole marriage deal had been a scam from the word go.

Pete never heard a word from Chris after that. He too disappeared, poor bugger.

VENEZUELA – BANDIT COUNTRY

Arrival in Caracas

I remember my first trip to Venezuela coinciding with the coalition forces attacking Iraq after Saddam Hussein had invaded Kuwait. In my mind, that period marked the start of when the modern world as I knew it really started going belly-up.

I remember Venezuela from school geography as a country on the other side of the world that sounded incredibly exotic. With a population around half of the UK's, largest oil reserves in the world, tropical paradise, jungles, deserted pristine beaches, the Llanos (grassy plains pronounced "yanos"), the flat-topped mountains (Tepuis) of the Gran Sabana and the Angel Falls, the highest waterfall in the world. Oh yes, almost forgot. Venezuela was also famous for its complete dominance of the Miss World contest for as long as I could remember. And if all that wasn't enough, you could apparently fill up your car's fuel tank for less than a quid! Seems like the country has it all. Let's go and see!

I travelled out from the UK on a direct flight from London, landing at Maiquetia airport in La Guaria, a coastal resort and major port area on the coast, just north of Caracas, Venezuela's Capital.

As we descended for landing, I remember being greeted not by a turquoise blue Caribbean colour-scape, but grey-green clouds and rain. Flaps and wheels down, out of the window I could see occasional glimpses of dark green mountains plunging dramatically into a somber grey sea. Red-brick shanty towns covered the lower slopes.

After what seemed like hours, I eventually got through immigration and customs, where my bag was searched by a sullen-faced National Guardsman who looked and acted like he had an IQ less than the bag he was searching.

Finally getting out of the air-conditioned terminal building into the tropical heat of Caracas, within seconds my shirt was soaked with sweat. Taking the first in line, I got into a huge, 1970's air-conditioned taxi, where the temperature suddenly went back to sub-zero and I immediately began to freeze.

Big old Chevrolet Malibu it was. The velvet interior smelled of cheap perfume and the rear wheels were each a good three inches wider than the wheel arches. The driver fired up the the enormous V8 engine and we rumbled and swayed away from the terminal, salsa music blaring out of the stereo.

The road from the airport up to Caracas was a winding highway of two lanes either way, separated by a three-foot high concrete barrier which was covered in black tyre marks and deep scratches. Hmmm.

The greasy black tarmac road had virtually no white lines and was packed with enormous old American gas-guzzling cars. Malibu's, Ford Fairlanes, with five, six litre engines, and ancient 16-wheeler trucks – the Venezuelans call them "Gandolas" - belching smoke as they crawled their way up to the capital.

There seemed to be no rules of the road, apart from the need to go as a fast as possible and get ahead of the car in front of you at all costs. The taxi, on its 1970 leaf-spring suspension and pulled by its enormous engine, wallowed and roared and weaved its way up the hill seemingly effortlessly. The driver flashed his headlights madly should anything slower appear in front of him.

We went up though several tunnels, some with lights, some without, and most with big lumps of the ceiling threatening to drop at any moment.

On entering the last tunnel, the uphill racetrack suddenly levelled off and then began dipping downwards. As we came back out into the bright sunlight, I was immediately confronted with Caracas in all its glory. Stunning blue skies overlying the most beautiful, dark green hills which formed an enormous East-West valley at the bottom of which nestled the city.

Someone told me that Caracas looks like a city that was built on a dark-green tablecloth, which some divine being had then lifted up by the edges. The city centre in the lower part of the valley had the usual tower blocks and high rise, but all the surrounding hillsides were covered with orange-brick shanty towns, often reaching the very summits. So densely packed were the shacks that it was hard to distinguish individual buildings. These were the so-called Ranchos.

Some of them were perched on concrete stilts so precarious it made you wonder how they could manage to stay there, let alone who would risk living in them. I was warned by many that these are areas not to be visited, either during the day or worse at night. Drug gangs, express kidnappings, lawlessness. Keep well clear.

I could fill this whole book on Venezuela, but I'll cut it short and limit it to the more entertaining moments. And yes, once again St. Christopher had to step in.

I'd been in the country for a couple of weeks, mostly exploring the deserted islands and coral reefs in the Morrocoy National Park, when I teamed up with a fellow who I'll call Dick and which, as it turned out, would have been an entirely appropriate name. He was pretty much doing the same as I was, bumming round the world and chanced his arm to see some of South America.

Lake Maracaibo and the Jeep

I'd heard about the snow-capped mountains south east of Lake Maracaibo over in the western part of the country. This was the northern extremity of the Cordillera – The Andes - which run from the very south of the Chile-Argentina border right up the west coast of the continent.

We hired a car and drove through the lush greenery of Maracay and Valencia, passing the arid brown hills of Barquisimeto and Carora, and eventually arrived at the hot, humid state of Zulia, and its capital city, Maracaibo. This was Western Venezuela's oil capital.

Seeing Lake Maracaibo for the first time is impressive. An inland sea some 80 miles wide and 120 miles north to south, it is fittingly shaped like a drop of oil. Quite shallow even in the middle, Lake Maracaibo is dotted with thousands of oil derricks, each on its own little square platform. Under each derrick was a beam-pump, or nodding donkey, sedately pumping oil from the thousands of wells below its surface.

Zulia state is one of the three large oil producing regions in Venezuela. They've pumped out so much oil from the southern part of the lake that the ground has sunk below sea level to such an extent that they have had to build a huge dyke some 30 feet high to keep the lake at bay. The coastal town of Lagunillas is below sea level.

Dick and I shacked up with some contacts in a place called Cuidad Ojeda, a dirty little oil town on the south east of the lake, complete with all the facilities you'd expect from a dirty little oil town. Bars, brothels, more bars, a few restaurants (loose description), a lot more brothels! Oh yes, and the Hotel America, the largest building in the town centre which was, in my opinion, not much more than a large bar and multi-storey brothel.

All the oil supply companies had their bases in Ojeda in order to provide the services for the thousands of wells on the lake and the surrounding shoreline.

As you can imagine, there were a lot of foreigners, all come to make it rich in the oil fields. Hundreds of supply shops lined the dusty main drag, stifling in the heat and the humidity and continually bombarded with non-stop merengue (pron. Meren-gay) and salsa music blasting out everywhere. The backdrop was completed by the ever-present burble of V8 engines and the smell of oil from the lake.

After a few days in Ojeda, which was plenty of time to realize that a few days was far too long, we were itching to continue our trip up into the Andes. Cold, fresh air, mountains and an entirely different face of Venezuela.

We were most definitely eager to get out of the cauldron of Cuidad Ojeda and had been told of a place called Los Frailes (pronounced Los Fry-laze), an ancient seventeenth century monastery nestling in a valley, high up above the clouds and which had been converted into a small hotel.

Apparently, the drive was about one hundred and fifty miles from Ojeda, climbing high almost to the snow line, hairpin bends with no guard rails and drops of thousands of feet to the river valleys below. Sounded awesome.

But we had a problem. No wheels! We checked out the local rentals, but they were far too expensive for our budget. Plus, we only wanted a one way-ride; we didn't intend to come back to Cuidad Ojeda. On top of that, most of the rental cars on offer didn't look like they'd make it out of the front gate.

We considering taking the bus, but figured we'd need St. Christopher and his entire family to look out for us. Seemingly without options, dis-illusionment soon started to set in.

Then, one afternoon in a bar, we got talking to a French fellow. Oil worker of course, who just happened to be ending his contract. He'd been there for two years in Ojeda and, guess what? He was selling an open-topped Renegade Jeep.

Beer's were finished and we went with him to see it, close by in the oil compound where he lived, right on the lake shore.

The Jeep was a real shit-box but looked mechanically sound enough. Black, with a great yellow stripe down the middle, enormous knobby Wrangler tyres, four-wheel drive, bloody great rollbar, and a 5 litre V8 engine under the hood. Starting it up, it sounded like a Sherman Tank.

The cockpit was basic to say the least. Apart from being filthy and half full of sand, it had two ripped, stained plastic front seats, no seat belts to speak of, a decayed bench seat in the back with a luggage space behind filled with all sorts or crap, including an empty gas tank, bits of fishing kit, and an old ice box. No canopy for the roof and certainly no air conditioning. To cap it all, strapped to the top and supported by the windscreen at the front and the rollbar at the back, was a well-used windsurfer.

"I use eem to go to zuh beach" the Frenchman told us.

No kidding.

"It goes OK, but zuh – how you say? - gear-stick sometimes he get steef, and zuh brakes, sometime you need pumping".

He threw us the keys and told us to take eet for a drive round zuh compound, which we did. Even though it really was a piece of shit, we had a hard job concealing our delight, especially as we figured on going to the

163

beach after the mountains. A deal was made and a handful of hundred-dollar bills were passed over right there and then.

"What about transfer of ownership? Papers?" we inquired.

Our French friend squeaked open the dash compartment door and fished out a dusty plastic wallet which looked like it had never seen the light of day in years. The paperwork inside looked like papyrus.

"If zuh police he stop you, just give him some Bolivares – zat is all zey want".

"Insurance?" The Frenchman gave us a look that suggested we need to realize this is not Europe. "'Ave a good time, mes amis!" And he winked and left.

Dick and I spent the next week rebuilding the entire braking system, doing a complete service, a new spare tyre, the full Monty. This was as challenging as it was entertaining, as neither of us could speak Spanish. Whilst we knew we were being ripped off at every turn, the local Venezuelans were a friendly bunch, and always, at any time of the day, ready for a few ice cold Polars. Polar was the most widely drunk Venezuelan beer.

All the Zulianos (blokes that is) seemed to have big bellies, all were dark brown, sweaty, all had moustaches, and all seem to be obsessed by baseball, beer and women.

Their vocabulary, although far too fast for us to understand, seemed to center around four words, which we found out were all obscenities. Anything you say was immediately met with a "No joda" (Pron: no hoh-duh), "verga" (Pron. Bear-guh) "Vaina" (Vy-nuh) or "que molleja (pronounced kay mo-yeca).

If you ever go to Maracaibo, in fact Venezuela in general, with these four words you can probably get by. And if you want to know what they mean, the closest I can get after consulting various linguistic experts are "No Joda" means "Fuck me!" as in the sense of "get away with you", "Verga" is "Prick", as in the prick meaning, "Vaina" has no translation at all but you can refer to anything with it, and "Que molleja" translates best as "You're shitting me" as in the "no kidding" sense. There you have it, you can now speak Venezuelan.

So, after a week of blood, sweat, tears and plenty of Polar beer, the two proud paperless owners of a black Renegade Jeep were ready for the mountains. At least as ready as the Jeep was ever going to be. All the lights were now working, which meant we were probably a unique vehicle in Venezuela. She looked pretty good, even the inside had been cleaned, and we'd loaded up with the sort of spares we figured we might need, although the ice box and a twenty-gallon Jerry can did take up most of the room.

Our bags were lashed to one side in the luggage compartment under a tarpaulin to stop them getting nicked at traffic lights, should we be foolish enough to stop at any. Such practice, especially after dark, wasn't recommended.

"If you see a breakdown on the road, dead bodies lying in the road, don't stop – it's a scam, you'll get robbed". Hmmm....a few patches of doubt were starting to appear in the sunny skies of the trip to the mountains of Venezuela.

At this point, I'll mention that Venezuela was and is a violent place, even back then. You needed to take care all the time. There was a lot of crime, gun crime, and the drug problem of today hadn't even started. Police and the infamous Guardia Nacional were as crooked as anyone, always ready to stop you to eke out a bribe. Oh yes, and druken driving, extremely druken driving that is, was the norm. Especially at night.

Los Frailes and the Bandits

So, the big day arrived, we said goodbye to our buddies in Cuidad Ojeda and pointed the Jeep south out of town, keeping the lake on our right.

Oil wells everywhere, the sounds and smells of Venezuela, the dark green hills, the orange baked earth, the sun beating down, baseball caps and ray-bans, ice-cold beer in hand (as mentioned, it was the norm) and the Jeeps' V8 burbling happily. Paradise. Oh yes, and we still had the windsurfer on top.

The plan was to drive up to the Monastery, stay a night or two, then head down the other side of the Cordillera along the coastal plain back to the beach to try out the windsurfer.

We'd been told to head south skirting the lake then start climbing into the mountains; it should take about ten hours to reach the monastery. No GPS of course, just a crappy fold-up map which was useless as it didn't seem to remotely correspond to the road network, and some hastily written notes on a scrap of paper.

What we didn't realize was that the time estimate of ten hours was based on the expat oil workers' experiences of driving at a hundred and twenty clicks an hour in fully loaded air-conditioned Land Cruisers, with local knowledge and being able to speak the local language. We had none of those advantages. Plus, we had a windsurfer and no roof.

We drummed along through towns and villages, oil rigs everywhere, through fires burning out of control along the road where people had lobbed their cigarette butts into tinder dry bush.

Enormous 18-wheeler gandolas plying their trade, stray dogs, dirty gas stations, roadside food stalls selling all sorts of stuff. The occasional check-point where, yes, we were customarily stopped for ten minutes whilst the men in the green uniforms tried to tell us we couldn't continue as we had no papers, but eventually let us go after us parting with a handful of Bolivares and a few cans of beer.

We ate roasted chicken from street vendors and drank ice-cold Polar beer. We got lost a few times, re-traced our steps, and tried to ask for directions which was a bit of a challenge when the only words you know are the equivalents of "Fuck me, Prick, Vaina and You're Shitting me!"

We stopped for fuel once, in a shitty Maraven gas station, typical of every gas station we saw. Full of 1970's old cars and trucks, people hawking all sorts of crap and fat, sweaty forecourt attendants in dirty orange overalls and flip-flops with their bare bellies sticking out.

There was always the obligatory tyre repair shop where everything and everyone was completely black in brake dust and oil. Wherever there were people, it was dirty, hot, humid and smelled of oil and smoked chicken. And had loud music.

Not three hours out of Ojeda, rumbling along at a steady fifty miles per hour, a new inconvenience appeared. The steering wheel came off in Dick's hand!

Now, having your steering wheel come off at fifty miles an hour is an enlightening experience, both for driver and passenger. Dick naturally braked and fortunately the Jeep veered to the right side of the road rather than the left and into the oncoming traffic.

The thread of the big central nut holding the wheel onto the column seemed to be worn out and Frenchie had obviously forgotten to tell us. We eventually managed to get the wheel back on the column, banging it home with a stone, but from then on, the driver had to apply continual forward pressure on it to keep it in place.

If this wasn't enough, the gear stick kept un-seating itself from the gearbox and, like the steering wheel, would come away in your hand. This was a fault we knew about and thought we had fixed, but obviously hadn't. The upside was that we wouldn't need to worry about the Jeep being nicked – we could simply take the gear lever and steering wheel with us if we did happen to leave it anywhere.

Anyway, as you can imagine, the initial euphoria of hitting the open road and adventure soon wore off. The constant boom from the engine and the tyres on the road, the back ache from the shitty seats and non-existent road signs meant that after about six hours, we hadn't a clue where we were and we were knackered.

For the last two hours we had been climbing, the road getting narrower by the kilometer and the villages getting poorer. The fact that we were going up made us figure we were going in the right direction.

We also noticed ominously that for each village that passed, we were getting more attention from the locals as we trundled by. These were mostly groups of blokes in sleevless vests, sporting sunglasses and gold chains and leaning on cars, drinking beer. Unnerving. In our innocence, we figured they were wondering why two gringos were going up the mountain with a windsurfer.

Then it started to get dark and, coupled with the increasing altitude, the temperature plummeted. We were now driving at well over seven thousand feet.

So, let's just recap the situation – it's now pitch black, open topped jeep, no heating, freezing cold, no idea where we were or how far to the destination, running low on fuel, narrow road with hairpin bends, no walls or safety barriers to stop you plummeting a thousand of feet down into a ravine, headlights that were pathetic, steering wheel that kept coming off, gear lever that kept coming out, and not another vehicle to be seen. It couldn't have gotten any worse.

In actual fact, it could.

The black 4x4 appeared from behind, catching us quickly and coming up close to our rear. It came so close it was almost pushing us. Even above the Jeep's engine we could hear the music booming out. In the little moonlight that occasionally appeared, we could see the car's windows seemed to be tinted and that's when we realized that we were probably the perfect target - Gringos, windsurfer, jeep, dollars, cameras - a good haul.

I was driving and yelled across to Dick, who looked like Lawrence of Arabia with an old rag round his head and neck to ward off the cold. "What weapons have we got?".

He leaned over and rummaged in the back and came back with a windsurfer mast-foot. That's a flexible, chunky piece of plastic about eighteen inches long that joins the mast to the board on a windsurfer. It could be used as a club! You kidding? A bit more rummaging produced a tyre lever. That's more like it.

Wearing three pairs of socks on my hands to ward off the frostbite, I tried to speed up. However, it was completely futile as there was was no chance of losing the 4x4, and we were already risking death at every curve from the thousand-foot vertical drop on our left.

No barriers, no white lines, just a dusty, gravel-strewn road which was slippery at the best of times. It was a death-trap at slow speed, but we were now going far, far too fast, adrenalin pumping from the prospect of the bandits behind.

Our pursuers were now trying to get level, taking more risks at every go. I was keeping to the middle of the

170

road, which wasn't difficult as it was barely wide enough for two vehicles. There were no straight stretches more than fifty yards long, and the road surface was now covered with more loose stones and the occasional patch of streaming water coming down from the vertical rock face on the right. This wouldn't be for the faint-hearted in the daylight!

We boomed along, the bandit's 4x4 seemingly tied to the back of our Jeep, sometimes making a bid to go down the side of us and which I fought off by swerving into their way. We were terrifed.

Suddenly, the Jeep's headlights picked out what seemed to be the end of the road, but which was in fact a hard-right hairpin. I yanked on the wheel as hard as I could, which caused it to pop clean off the steering column. We had five yards before we were going airborne! FUUUUUUUUUUCCKKKKKK!!!!!

With the front wheels a yard from the edge I jammed on the brakes, slammed the wheel back in, wrenched hard right again and St. Christopher pushed the Jeep back onto the road and around the corner. I swear we must have had the wheels over the edge. It could only have been Him.

Now careering towards the next bend, the Baddies had dropped back probably because they must have hit the back of the jeep when we braked hard. If they did, they probably came out worse; we didn't even feel it. The Jeep's engine boomed, Dick was yelling something intelligible at the top of his voice and to complicate matters even more, the fuel gauge was now showing empty.

The narrow, winding road was our saviour, as the Baddies couldn't get past us, and it looked like they were   keeping a bit of a distance in case we decided to brake again. One side was a vertical wall of rock upwards, the other a vertical drop hundreds of feet down into the blackness.

Unfortunately, these natural defences suddenly started to look in doubt. The road had started to slope downwards, the curves becoming less dramatic and worst of all, the road was also starting to widen. It would only be a matter of time before they would attempt another pass.

I now had the jeep at full throttle, slaloming from side to side as we hurtled down through the blackness, with no chance to stop in the fifty feet or so that the headlights gave us. I kept pushing like hell on the steerting wheel to stop it coming off, driving almost standing up. Suddenly it was the turn of the gear lever to come off again.   All the shaking had obviously loosened the retaining screw to the point that allowed it to pop out of its socket of its own accord and fell into the footwell. I don't know to this day how I managed it, but before it bounced out of the door, I made a wild lunge down between my legs and managed to grab it. I quickly passed it to Dick shouting "Chuck this at their windscreen!" completely oblivious the implications of having no gear stick from then on.

Dick half stood up and turned to take aim, his Lawrence of Arabia headgear flapping violenty in the slipstream.

We were now hurtling along at some 70 miles an hour, driving on adrenalin and fumes as the baddies made another gambit to come along side. Dave suddenly looked across at me with a terrified face and yelled "They've got a gun!"

He could see an arm out of one window holding what looked like, and most definitely was, a gun. The road was barely wide enough for both vehicles, but our advantage was we didn't give a shit about our paintwork. I swung on the wheel again to block the attack and the chasers dropped back again. A sharp crack and a flash sounded above the roaring of the engine. "Holy Shit! The bastards are shooting at us!"

Dave dived down into the passenger footwell and I tried to make myself as small as possible whilst keep the pressure on the steering wheel and trying to see where we were going.

Suddenly, about five hundred yards ahead I spotted a small light, and the road seemed to be a dead straight line leading to it. I pressed harder on the accelerator pushing the Jeep now well beyond its mechanical limits. We had exceeded its safe limits a long time ago.

The fast approaching lights up ahead started to show that it was a white building and suddenly a sign shot by advising us of "Hotel Los Frailes" to the left!

"It's the Monastery!" screamed Dick. Holy shit, we were almost there!

But now, the road had widened and the more powerful 4x4 behind sensed a kill. They were coming up fast. This time we saw the gun clearly pointing towards us!

Leaving it to the last possible moment and using all the experiences of Fast Courier driving, I slammed on the brakes, locking up all four wheels. We went from probably eighty miles per hour to almost nothing in a matter of seconds causing the windsurfer to shoot forward and drop at an angle over the bonnet. The bandits, almost level at that point, were caught completely by surprise and they shot past, the gunman withdrawing his arm to avoid losing it against the side of the jeep.

I hauled on the wheel as we slewed sideways into the Monastery's entrance drive, Dick yelling obscenities at the bandits who were now a good hundred yards further down the road. Their brake lights were on, they slowed for few seconds but then obviously realizing we had turned into a safe haven, probably thought better of it and disappeared out of sight into the blackness.

We slewed into what was probably a car park still going at forty miles an hour, and I slammed on the brakes again, desperately trying to stop the two-ton jeep from demolishing the hotel.

At that moment, the engine coughed and spluttered and died. No fuel! And no engine meant no power assistance for the brakes and no power for the steering, which immediately went rock-solid. We ploughed straight through a hedge and went ten yards up what appeared to be a grass bank before finally shuddering to a stop.

As a final gesture, the jeep then rolled silently backwards down into the car park and stopped, the engine pinging and hissing and smelling of burnt oil.

We both sat there staring ahead without saying a word, breathing heavily for what seemed an eternity. Then, slowly we both got out, peered at each other in the semi-darkness, still shaking from the excitement and burst out laughing. Me with a steering wheel in my hands and Dick with a gear lever and a rubber mast foot.

At this point a security guard appeared from the direction of the hotel torch in hand and flashed it over the scene. He didn't actually say anything - I don't think he had ever seen anything like this before.

You can imagine his face being confronted by a wreck of a black jeep with a windsurfer hanging over the bonnet and two gringos wrapped up like Bedouins, each holding a selection of car parts in their hands. In the middle of the night.

"Buenos noches" I said, grinning like I'd just come first place in the Monte Carlo Rally. We grabbed our bags and walked up to Reception.

"Ah, Señor Ballantinny. We were worreed" said the receptionist, an elderly fellow with a smile.

"You were fucking worried? Que Molleja!" I thought. It had taken us fifteen hours and we were lucky to be alive.

Formalities over, the warm welcoming reception, the smiling receptionist, it was a matter of minutes before I was in my room. I sat on the bed and started shaking. In the mirror, what looked like a first-world war pilot stared back at me. I then looked up at the ceiling and murmured a quiet thanks to St. Chris.

After showering, we found the restaurant, and after the first beer I got an attack of something. Don't know if it was delayed sunstroke, altitude sickness, or post-traumatic stress syndrome, but whatever it was, I pretty much passed out.

Dick, the lucky sod, told me later that he'd enjoyed a huge steak, washed down with a bottle of Chilean red wine, and had spent the evening chatting up the barmaid.

The following morning, I felt better, and ate a hearty breakfast and went for a walk. The place was stunning. The monastery a beautiful example of old South American architecture, complete with a bell tower which was illuminated at night. A crystal clear, blue sky, mountains that were totally virgin, and waterfalls running from thousands of feet, carving valleys through the spectacular vegetation of the Andean foothills. There were no sounds, just a breeze and the songs of a few birds. For me, it could have been a place where God lived, as he or one of his buddies had surely given us a helping hand in getting there. Worth a visit, for sure.

Anyway, time wasn't on our side, so next day we loaded up, managed to buy a liter of fuel off the hotel, checked out, replaced the steering wheel and gear lever as best we could, and, keeping our eyes open for dodgy looking cars with blacked out windows, we literally free wheeled six thousand feet to the first fuel station. In fact, it was a guy who had a Gerry can - but it was enough. We paid him handsomely in dollars.

This had been a trip to remember.

Canaima and Salto Sapo

This tale is about one of the most amazing places on earth. The Gran Sabana and the Angel Falls in Venezuela.

As this is not a travel book, I thought about leaving this trip out as nothing out of the ordinary happened. However, I guess the reason I have included it is simply due to how totally awesome the place was. On this adventure, I really did feel like Indiana Jones, travelling there twenty-five years ago, flying over the green carpet of the jungle forests of Southern Venezuela in an old Douglas Dakota.

It was the last few days of the Venezuela trip, and I was still in the company of Dick, although the relationship had become pretty fraught. We were simply different, and I think that whilst I looked back on the mountain pursuit by bandits with a laugh, Dick seemed to have gone a lot quieter after the near-death experience. After all, Dick had never worked for Fast Courier.

Amazing how, when you are used to being single and completely answerable to yourself only, that another party very quickly becomes a pain in the ass. Whilst I was more and more convinced Dick really was a Dick, I must admit I was pretty whacky in those days and it must have been a challenge to keep up with me.

We also had teamed up with a girl who was working in the British Embassy in Caracas and who we had met in a bar one night. Jenny had a few days off and was keen to see the Angel Falls, so it seems being in the company of two seemingly decent, single British blokes sounded a good bet to her.

We had taken a fifty-minute scheduled flight from Caracas to Cuidad Bolivar (Bolivar City), with a view to staying there overnight before taking a flight south to the Canaima National Park the following morning.

Cuidad Bolivar is on the southern bank of the mighty Orinocco River, at one of its narrowest points where the river was just under a mile wide. Being the point of one of the few major bridges crossing the river, Cuidad Bolivar was previously called Angostura, famous for the creation of Angostura Bitters. Angostura means "narrowing" in Spanish.

The town is also the gateway to the Gran Sabana (the Great Sheet), the vast unpopulated expanse of tropical forests, rivers, waterfalls and flat-topped mountains called Tepuis, that stretch down to the Amazon and Brazil.

The Gran Sabana is the backdrop used in Arthur Conan Doyle's "Lost World". The Canaima National Park is part of the Gran Sabana and it was there that we were headed, to see the Angel Falls, the highest waterfall in the world.

Now, there was me thinking maybe it was me. But soon, Dick and Jenny were not seeing eye to eye either, so it must've been Dick, and not me. The tensions became such that Dick jumped ship and flew back to Caracas the following day. So, with the adage of two's company well proven, a happy Jenny and yours truly were off on an adventure.

Cuidad Bolivar hadn't had much to offer. Probably very nice in its colonial hey-day, it was pretty run down, and we were advised not to wander around at night. We didn't.

We were up early the following day eager for adventure. The airport terminal only just qualified for the title, as it was very basic, no air conditioning, humid as hell, with a few bored-looking officials hanging around. And of course, the odd Guardia Nacional official on the look -out for someone he could shake down.

The check-in counter was nothing more than a wooden desk behind which sat an enormously fat lady on a fold-up chair. Nothing automated, paper tickets, hand-written boarding pass. The whole place had an air of "nothing's happening, and nothing will" about it. Wonderful.

There was a small kiosk selling all sorts of cheap souvenir shit which didn't interest us, but it did sell beer, so we cooled off waiting for the flight to be announced. It soon was, by a fellow in a loosely fitting overall sticking his head round a door which evidently led to the tarmac, and yelling "Canaima" at the top of his voice. We aimed for the door.

Out into the tropical heat, we walked out across a sun-baked apron to a great big, twin engined Douglas Dakota, or DC3. Stuff of legends! I'm convinced the airline had borrowed it off the filmset of The Wild Geese. It was magnificent!

As the Dakota was a tail dragger, meaning it's third wheel is at the back, below the tail, and the whole fuselage points to the sky when the plane is on the ground. We climbed up the short steel ladder into the small back door, where the parachutists would have bailed out over Northern France in World War Two! The seats were benches along each side of the plane, one side facing the other. The windows had obviously been modified and were much bigger than usual, presumably to give the punters a panoramic view.

We expected to be pretty much the only passengers due to the apparent lack of people in the terminal, but obviously with local knowledge that nothing was going to happen on time, the plane slowly filled up with all manner of folk, all locals. It took me straight back to Peru. There were live animals, babies crying, people smoking, plastic cups of hooch passing up and down. It seemed we were the only tourists, and to this day I can't remember if we had seat belts on.

The back door was closed, the engines spluttered then thundered into life, the plane trundled to the runway, and with a deafening roar, the Dakota picked up speed, the back end came up and we lifted off. I was in heaven. This was my kind of flying.

As we climbed, the vista below was breathtaking. I felt like we were flying over a deep, green, shag-pile carpet. Every so often, a brown river would snake its way through this carpet, the edges immaculately precise. After twenty minutes or so, in the distance, rising out of this paradise, we saw the first of the Tepuis. Table-top mountains, vertical sides, falling hundreds, even thousands of feet to the forest below. Their flat plateau summits were covered in vegetation apparently hiding species which are still unknown to man today.

The Tepuis are known as islands in the sky, as the mists often cover the green forests below and the Tepuis rise above like immense buildings emerging out of a grey-white sea. The climate and fauna on top are completely different from the green forest carpet below.

It's off one of these Tepui's, the Auyantepui, that the Angel Falls cascade two thousand, six hundred and forty-eight feet down into the jungle below.

In all my travels, flying over that green carpet in an old Dakota, and seeing the Gran Sabana in all its glory is without doubt one of my most incredible and unforgettable memories.

After about an hour's flight, which seemed like five minutes due to the awesome distraction of the Gran Sabana, we landed at Canaima, part village and part tourist destination on the banks of the River Carrao.

Canaima was basically a staging post for the Angel Falls, and the reason why tourists went there. As the plane comes into land, you get a bird's eye view of enormous rivers, lagoons and a myriad of large waterfalls. Breathtakingly beautiful. (Google "Images for Canaima" and you'll see what I mean).

The Dakota rumbled to a stop and for the first time in my life I was actually sorry to get off an aeroplane.

Disembarking, the passengers all went their separate ways, either on foot or picked up by a variety of mostly crapped-out vehicles which had been waiting beyond the concrete apron.

The airstrip had certainly seen better days, with a small control tower which probably hadn't seen a lick of paint since it was built, a few huts and containers and a motley collection of single and twin-engined planes in various states of dis-repair. Some even had the engines missing. The whole place oozed abandonment, even though it was one of the main tourist destinations of Venezuela.

We were transported by a beat-up Toyota Land Cruiser down a muddy road to a collection of three or four thatched huts, behind which was the river. This was the resort. There was a small shop which also served as a tourist information office.

Walking in between two of the huts, we were suddenly faced with the most incredible sight of the Carrao river in all it's glory. It was truly breathtaking. An off-white sandy beach gave way to what appeared to be a large bay of glistening, moving water, blue at a distance, but red-brown close up. Not the murky brown of muddy water, but a clear transparent brown, like tea without milk. This colouring comes from tannins which enter the rivers upstream from a leeching process of the forest. It's brown, but perfectly drinkable.

Away to the right, about two hundred meters away, a waterfall, probably some hundred yards wide, thundering water into the bay. The stunning beauty is hard to describe. All you could hear was the distant roar of the waterfall, the chirping of birds and the lapping of the water on the beach. We just stood on the sand and stared in awe. Once again, Mother Nature at her absolute finest.

Reverie broken, we went to the "reception" and were assigned a grass-roofed hut. We dumped our bags and went straight out, eager to explore. Hot and sticky, I stripped off to my shorts and ran into into the river for a swim. It was deliciously cool. I tried swimming to the falls, but the current against me was too strong. Getting back to the beach, Jenny had found a local guide who offered to take us up-river behind the falls.

Dried off, we followed the guide for about twenty minutes walking through the forest bordering the river, and after climbing up a steep incline, we appeared at the top of the same falls we had seen from the beach.

The noise, the spray and the sheer power of the water and the wind it generated were exhilarating. However, the guide, in the few words of English he could manage, gesticulated for us to follow him away from the falls and continue up-river along the bank.

We soon came to a long canoe with a small outboard motor, tied to the bank. We clambered in and the guide pulled the engine to life and we turned and pointed upriver, the sun blazing overhead, the cool river rushing past us.

The cleared banks quickly became deep undergrowth and after about ten minutes we turned sharply left and entered what seemed to be another tributary, no bank as such, just dense foliage overhanging into the tannin water. We were now going with the current and picked up sufficient speed to create quite a cooling breeze in our faces.

Five minutes or so later, the foliage on the banks disappeared and the river seemed to open out into a collection of different channels, with one main flow in the centre. The guide manoeuvered the boat to the edge and tied it to a rock. We clambered out and followed him, carefully picking our way over wet, mossy rocks protruding from the rushing water.

We could see now that the river in front of us simply disappeared, the clouds of spray beyond the edge warning of another waterfall. The guide led us at right-angles away from it to a muddy path, into deep undergrowth and which we followed for about one hundred meters, the sound of thundering water getting louder with every step.

All of a sudden, we came out of the bushes and only a few yards in front of us was an enormous wall of water, thundering down from about a hundred feet above our heads and crashing down into a maelstrom of spray way below us. We couldn't see the bottom for the clouds of spray.

We had emerged approximately halfway down the fall and the noise was deafening, the spray enveloping us and the wind from the millions of gallons of water falling a few feet from our faces was unbelievable. In a matter of seconds, we were soaked to the skin. This was Salto Sapo, or the Frog Waterfall.

We saw the guide had produced a black plastic bin-liner. "Cameras" he said, pointing in turn to our cameras and the bag. Understanding what he wanted, but not really why, we passed over our valuables and he wrapped them up tightly. "Come" he said. "Follow. Hold rope strong!"

184

As we watched, the path and the guide disappeared into the waterfall! I grabbed Jenny's hand and we stepped forward into the maelstrom. My hand felt a rope fastened to the rock face and I turned and yelled at Jenny to grab it.

We inched forward. I don't know which was the stronger sensation, the almost darkness, the cold wind, the clouds of blinding spray, the thunderous noise, or the impenetrable wall of blue-brown water thundering downwards a foot off my right shoulder. I put one finger in it and it was nearly torn off. Imagine going in that.

This was very scary stuff. My worry was for Jenny who was right behind me. The rock floor we were inching along was very uneven and extremely slippery and visibilty was virtually nil. There came one point where there was a fairly heavy fall of water we had to actually pass through. We clung to the rope for dear life and inched forward.

It seemed like ages before we emerged out at the other side. There was the guide, calmly sitting on a rock in the warm sunshine, eating a banana.

Jenny and I emerged from the fall soaked to the skin, cold, shaking and absolutely euphoric! The grin on our faces just wouldn't go away.

As we turned and looked back, the noise seemed to diminish, the sun dried us in a matter of minutes, and we had a view of the falls from the other side which was even better that the first.

Being this close to nature, feeling and tasting it was truly exhilarating.

After we had dried out and taken some pictures, the guide said questioningly "Go back?" and pointed first back through waterfall and then to what was a rocky path snaking up this side of the falls.

Jenny pointed immediately up the path.

We returned to the village and paid off the guide, thanking him profusely.

That night we had a basic but tasty meal in a little shack close to the huts, and crashed out, tired from the day's exertions, and lulled to sleep by the sound of nature. Next day…. the Angel Falls.

The Angel Falls

The next morning, after a simple, but delicious breakfast of black beans, fried platano and arepa, a maize doughnut without the hole which formed the staple diet of the Venezuelans, we walked up through the village to the airstrip and looked for our plane.

We showed our voucher to a fellow who was dressed like a mechanic and he pointed to a jaded, white and brown Cessna 172 with the engine cowling up and a large black arse sticking out of it. As we walked over, seeds of doubt were beginning to appear.

We approached with the statutory "Buenos dias", and the black ass backed down the step and turned to greet us, turning into a large dark-skinned man who introduced himself. "Cap-ee-tan Gonzalez, Señores!"

I did the best I could not to laugh out loud! He was a splendid looking fellow, big and beefy, jet-black hair slicked back, an impressive handlebar moustache, and dressed as if he normally flew 747's for British Airways. Epaulets, gold braid everywhere, metallic badges, the lot.

His English was enough to hold a basic conversation. "Weather good. You lucky. We go in five minutes. You go toilet? Two-hour trip".

Our shaking heads prompted the invitation to board, as he banged the engine cowling shut and wrenched open a door below the wing which looked as if it might come off in his hand. So bizarre was the whole scenario, I was half expecting to find a dozen black mambas in the cockpit, and a baddie with an eye-patch pointing a Luger at me.

As we settled tightly next to each other into our seats, I took a quick check of the inside. Not the cleanest plane I've ever been in, most of the perspex windows were cracked, one door handle was held on by some tape, the seatbelts looked like they'd never been used, and most concerning of all, the dashboard had several gaping holes in it where presumably instruments were supposed to be.

Jenny and I exchanged glances, but before we could say anything, Captain Gonzalez clambered aboard and maneouvered his substantial bulk into the front seat. "No co-pilot today. He sick" and our Captain made a mime of drinking from a bottle and laughed hoarsely.

Gonzalez then started throwing switches and twiddling dials for at least five minutes, switching things on and off and furiously tapping more than one of the dials. I could see it was the fuel gauges, and the needle wasn't budging from empty. After a while, he gave up, the dial still reading empty, and he started the engine which groaned, groaned again then spluttered into life. The little Cessna began to rock.

"Hey! One come sit front" shouted Captain Gonzalez over his shoulder as put on a headset. I noticed that the cable's end was hanging on the floor as I scrambled forward and squeezed myself into the copilot's seat.

Curious this, and as I have said many times in this book, I am terrified of flying. But not like this. Even with the dodgy pilot, the missing gauges, a plane that has probably not seen a maintenance hangar in years, it was just glorious. I was having the time of my life.

Gonzalez gunned the engine and the Cessna wobbled forward towards the end of the runway. Without even looking for incoming flights, he lined us up and applied full power.

Over two hundred meters the Cessna picked up speed and suddenly we were airborne, climbing slowly into the morning sunlight, the lake and waterfalls over to our left looking stunning.

The concrete of the runway left us, and we were immediately over the thick carpet of dense, green jungle. The thought of having only one engine crossed my mind, but the sights were just too awesome to be able to think about anything else. Endless green jungle as far as the eye could see, interlaced with winding rivers, blue-brown or blinding silver when the sun reflected on their surface.

After about half an hour or so, flying at some two and half thousand feet – yes, the altimeter seemed to work – we were fast approaching a vertical rock face. This was the north side of the AuyánTepui, the island in the sky which was the source of the Angel Falls.

Instead of increasing altitude and flying above, Gonzalez banked left, and we skirted the rock face, maybe a couple of hundred feet below the top. It was awesome, the sheer cliff plunging vertically from far above us down into the forest far below.

There was not a cloud in the sky and the view was spectacular. All around we could see other Tepui's, miles away, all appearing to be of exactly the same height, all flat-topped as if machined to size. And in between these islands, the perfect green carpet.

We continued banking round the Tepui, both me and Jenny completely awestruck, each with our own thoughts, silently taking pictures which we knew would never be able to do justice to the sight before us.

Suddenly Captain Gonzalez started gesticulating and pointing, and there it was. The Angel Falls.

Named after Jimmy Angel, a US flyer who in the fifties was the first person to fly over the falls, and who's ashes were scattered on the top of the Tepui, the falls are the highest free-fall of water in the world, a small volume river which plunges almost three thousand feet down a vertical rock face to the forest below. So high is the fall, that on its way down the water turns into mist. We were lucky in that there was good volume of water and the sky was clear blue. Often the Tepui is shrouded in clouds, or, in the dry season, the volume of water is very low. Today was perfect.

Gonzalez circled around three of four times, took the Cessna up above the top pf the plateau and after some twenty minutes, which actually seemed a lot longer, he gave the thumbs up, pointed at the empty fuel gauge and banked the plane round back towards Canaima.

The trip back to Canaima, back to Cuidad Bolivar and back to Caracas where I'd catch my flight back to the UK was uneventful, but crushingly depressing. Leaving the Gran Sabana left me with a feeling of having been close to the origins of the earth, the beginning of time, almost as if this was another planet.

In Caracas airport I said goodbye to Jenny, both promising to keep in touch, and which neither of us did. Perhaps if Facebook had been around then we might have.

Footnote

In 1999, Hugo Chavez became President of Venezuela, introducing a socialist doctrine that has continued to this day, even after his death in 2013. Almost twenty years of corrupt attempts at extreme socialism has bankrupted the country and left millions of Venezuelans, those who could not flee the country, in extreme poverty.

As I write, there are no medicines, virtually no food unless you buy on the black market, staggering inflation, crime rates are off the charts and Venezuela has become a failed state.

There is no end in sight to the totalitarian government's grip pf power, and it is said that they are now offering dubious mining contracts to Chinese and Russian companies in the pristine and once-protected national park of Canaima. Corruption and violence are rife.

The Venezulean Oil Industry, once one of the best in the world, has been completely crippled.

A country that could be paradise on earth has being virtually destroyed.

I am only glad that I managed to visit when it was possible.

BARBEEDOS

During the years I worked in the exhibitions business, I met a guy at one of the events who owned a small bungalow in Barbados. I had been working my balls off for the previous four months of the summer, pretty much non-stop, seven days a week, often as much as eighteen hours a day. I was completely knackered and really in need of a rest.

As I'd never been to the Caribbean, Barbados sounded just what the doctor ordered, so, after making a deal with this fellow, I booked a week's vacation to coincide with a quiet period prior to the London Motor Show in October. A good rest was essential prior to the ten days of mayhem that was the Motor Show, even without considering the previous four months slog!

Off to the sun

A small shoulder bag with basic items and paperback in hand, I flew alone, British Airways direct from London. I remember the curious sideways glances from the suit-cased tourists at check-in.

The flight was uneventful apart from being long, and the view as we descended to the turquoise Caribbean and glimpses of snow-white beaches soon uplifted my spirits and left London far behind.

Getting off the plane, I was immediately caressed by the warm Caribbean breeze, eyes half shut due to the extreme brightness of the brilliant blue sky. It was such a change from the grey, cold drizzle I had left ten hours before. As I got off the plane down the portable steps to the tarmac, the thought of never going back came into my head - a thought I was to have many times in the future.

I walked the fifty yards to the quaint terminal building in single file with the other happy passengers, mostly couples of varying ages, and all remarkably white. A week later, the same folks would be getting back on the plane the colour of cooked lobsters.

Inside the terminal, the soft sound of Calypso music reminded you of exactly where you were, in case you had drunk too much on the flight and were in any doubt. The whole experience was relaxed, pleasant, un-rushed, un-crowded, and everyone seemed to be happy. And colourful. Contrastingly opposite to Heathrow where everyone seemed to be in a rush, dressed in black and looking miserable.

I walked up to the immigration desk, first in the queue as I wasn't taking happy snaps outside like everyone else, got my passport stamped by an enormous, jovial lady with skin the colour of pitch and who welcomed me to Barbeedos. As I had no bags, I walked straight through customs and emerged into the almost empty arrivals hall.

Following the signs towards the taxi rank, I suddenly spotted my name scrawled in felt pen on a piece of paper. I didn't know it, but my friend had organized for someone to pick me up at the airport.

An enormous row of white teeth in a jet-black face introduced themselves as Adrian (that's Eeed-ree-un) and welcomed me to Barbeedos again. I followed him out of the terminal to his small micro-bus. I clambered in and it immediately became apparent I was to be the only passenger as Adrian started the engine.

Adrian had obviously been briefed on how to make me feel welcome, as he opened a small cooler and passed me an ice-cold beer. He had one himself too.

The bus coughed to life and we rattled out of the airport and set off through the lush greenery of Barbados, every once and a while having glimpses of the translucent turquoise Caribbean.

The colour of the sea was so vivid it almost seemed unreal, like a TV set with the colour turned up too much. Adrian said he'd take the long way around to show me a bit of the island's south coast. I was in no hurry. In paradise you don't need to hurry.

Within an hour after of landing, I had seen a bunch of stunning white beaches, all with their own beach bars, seen where the golf course was, and driven past some of the more famous colonial buildings. See how far you get one hour from landing in a foreign country today - you'll most likely still be in immigration or be still waiting for your suitcase!

We eventually pulled up outside a small, quaint yellow house in an overgrown, but enchanting garden. Home for the next week. Adrian drove away after giving me a few local tips and offering to return in a couple of days to give me a more complete tour.

The bungalow was basic enough, wooden hoardings painted bright yellow, a terrace overlooking a small garden full of plants and brilliantly coloured flowers, with birds and insects busily chirping and buzzing, everything continually caressed by the warm Caribbean breeze.

Opening the rickety wooden front door, I stepped into a main living area, and off through other doors was a small kitchen, a couple of bedrooms and a bathroom. Wooden floors which creaked as you walked around. The wooden terrace had a couple of rattan chairs and there were hooks for a hammock which would no doubt be inside somewhere. Perfect. What more could you ask for?

There was no air conditioning, but the ceiling fan and the constant breeze kept things refreshingly cool. The nearest beach was only a five-minute walk.

This was paradise all right. That notion of not going back to Blighty was starting to grow again!

Having unpacked my gear, which took all of thirty seconds, I wandered out of the house feeling pretty tired after the long flight and time difference. It was around 6pm there, but early hours of the morning back in the UK. Knackered, yes, but still up for a sundowner (or was it down for a sun-upper?) Not too sure. Anyway, when I reached the beach, I could see a few hundred yards away a small resort that seemed to have a bar right on the beach. That'll do nicely.

I strolled along the beach enjoying the warm sand, feeling tremendously self-conscious of being the whitest person on display by far. The majority of folks were either dark brown or jet black, the locals, or pink or bright red which were the tourists. You did occasionally see a perfectly suntanned foreigner and I hoped I'd be that colour soon enough.

I reached the bar and there was an empty table looking over the sea. Absolutely stunning location, so I ordered a beer and a large seafood platter with extra prawns.

After Fast Courier in West London, after months of slog on the exhibition circuit driving trucks up and down the motorways of England in the traffic queues, the rain, the cold, working till God only knows what time of night, I suddenly had this incredibly relaxing feeling as if someone had suddenly pulled my battery out? Had I died? Was I in heaven? Was I turning into a Squid, similar to the one I had just shoved in my mouth? I sat there and reflected, really thinking that life at that moment was pretty bloody good. Single, healthy, good job, in Paradise and....Hello, Hello, ... two girls at the next table!

It didn't take long, or many drinks, before we were chatting, and one of the girls asked where was my wife? Apparently, nobody travels on their own. This would be the first time of many I have been asked that question.

"I don't have one" I replied, noting the cocktail-fuelled nods and winks between the two.

We continued talking, and it turned out that they were from Liverpool on a week's all-inclusive. They were obviously getting up a head of steam, and I was slowly getting lower and lower in my chair as the flight, the time difference and life so far caught up with me. With my eyes closing, I hauled myself to my feet and bid them goodnight, indicating that I'd be back tomorrow and happily add to their all-inclusive agenda. Nudge, nudge, wink, wink, say no more!

Meeting Mount Gay

The next morning, I awoke really early Barbados time, and was feeling pretty chipper after being unconscious for a good twelve hours.

So, I needed to get sorted. First things first – some wheels! A few blocks away was a rental place - very basic, which had been pointed out by Adrian. I never use the big multi-national rental agencies. Too expensive.

I hired a Mini-Moke. A bit like a normal mini that has had it's upper body sliced off horizontally just above the wheels. Can't really get more basic. Basically, a large, open topped go-kart with four seats which the British army used as rapid deployment vehicles by throwing them out of the back of transport planes on the end of a parachute.

So, with the transport sorted for the week, I was almost set for the beach. Next stop, 'Nick's Wine and Liquor Store". Adrian had warned me not to buy drinks at the beach bars as they were very expensive "Best get yourself an ice box and buy at the local stores". So I did.

The proprietor of "Nick's Wine and Liquor Store" was an extremely friendly Brit called John. I never found out why it wasn't "John's Wine and Liquor Store". Anyway, John gave some advice as to which beaches to use, and sold me a bottle of Mount Gay rum, a six pack of

Coke, a pack of plastic cups, and a bag of ice. I was all set. He also warned me to watch out for three things.

Firstly, the sun. In Barbados, you'll get burnt even if it's cloudy, which it wasn't. Secondly the beach hawkers – they'll steal anything, so watch your stuff. And third, Mount Gay Rum. Cheap local brew, easy to drink with Coke, but requires respect.

Thanking him for his help, I happily chucked the stuff in the back of the Moke and drove off to the first beach.

It was divine. Perfect white sand, almost like flour, virtually deserted as it was still fairly early, and a sea so turquoise you couldn't stop looking at it. The pleasantly warm onshore breeze provided a welcome antidote to the searing sun whilst gently rustling the palm tree fringe.

I walked a bit down the beach to the bar I had visited the night before and took the same table. I was actually after a good breakfast, but they didn't have anything I fancied, so, convincing myself it was past midday in the UK, I had another seafood platter, with a couple of beers to wash it down. Excellent.

Feeling fantastic, I wandered back up the beach away from the resort and found a quiet spot. I laid out a towel, got the Walkman out, treated myself to my first Mount Gay and Coke and dreamily lay down to enjoy total peace in Paradise, dreamily watching a catamaran slide by on the horizon.

By this time, I had made up my mind. That was it. I'm staying here and never going back to the UK.

My reverie was suddenly rudely interrupted by a deep voice.

"Eee, maan, du want yer 'air braidin'?

"What the f.....?" I half opened my eyes against the blazing sun and made out a bloody great black face staring down at me." Where the hell did he come from?"

Adjusting to the glare, the silhouette becomes a tall, lanky fellow, dreadlock hairdo, skin so black it was almost blue, clothes that looked like he'd been shipwrecked a year ago and holding a bag of beads and coloured bracelets.

"Eh?" was about all I could muster, as mixed emotions fought each other over this git invading my silence.

"Yuh want yer 'air braidin', mon?"

Do I want my friggin' hair braiding? Considering I'd had a number two buzz-cut all over before leaving London, he'd have to be a bloody magician or micro-surgeon and I figured he was either taking the piss or just being bloody annoying. It then became obvious this was an opening line prior to the offering of more shady wares.

"No, thanks" I said, trying to make it sound like an authoritarian "Piss off!".

I reckon the fellow saw something in my eyes which made him decide fairly quickly that I wasn't going to be convinced too easily, so he lifted his spaced-out gaze and sloped off along the beach in search of other prey.

I had another slurp of Mount Gay and Coke, closed my eyes again and relaxed back into the calming sounds of the deserted beach and lapping of the waves.

Two minutes later. "Woowoo, Aloe Vera man?"

"What, another one?" Even though I had no idea what he was trying to flog, this time I didn't even bother with the "err" and just growled "No".

Two minutes later.

"Eh man. 'ow aboot a bita de Ganga?" Hmm. Straight to the point this one.

"No thanks, mate" I said, maintaining an element of courtesy as this one looked a lot dodgier than the others. I still tried putting as much threat into my voice as possible.

And so on it went. Non-stop pestering. Perhaps this was why this section of the beach was deserted. I found out later that these fellows were working their way up the beach towards the bigger hotels, and I was close to their starting point. I remember being plagued by mosquitos on an island off Venezuela, but these buggers were something else.

Let's go water Skiing again

After a few hours of sun, two hundred visits from what seemed like the entire male population of Barbados under thirty years of age, the occasional swim, and an almost empty bottle of Mount Gay, I felt a spell of unconsciousness coming on. I rolled over, dug a pit in the sand, wrapped my valuables in my T-shirt, buried the bundle under the towel, and promptly fell asleep on top of it.

Before I knew it, and what seemed like only a couple of minutes later, someone was shaking my shoulder. I cracked my eyes open and squinted up at Bob Marley, version 201.

"Eh man, dyu wan' go de woter skiin'?"

Did I want to go water skiing? Eh? I didn't have a clue where I was, or who he was. I also felt like shit. My head throbbed and I hurt. All over.

As I slowly came to, I became aware of a burning sensation on one side of my face and body. I looked at my watch. I had been asleep for almost three hours. I reckon I had second degree burns on one side, head to toe, whilst the other side was like white sandpaper. The image of a red penguin came to mind.

"So, woter skiin' den?"

The burning sensation was so acute, I figured I needed to be in water- any water – pretty damn quick.

"How much" I croaked? He told me the price for twenty minutes, "Twenty-eet dollar, Marn", and I agreed. Marley's face lit up with a broad grin - a punter!

I staggered to my feet, feeling like I'd just come out of a pizza oven, immediately fell over, got back up and took in my surroundings. The beach was a lot busier now, couples and families spaced out at regular intervals, towels and sunbrellas marking each one's territory. As I staggered after Marley, I began to focus and could see that people were also starting to take notice of a Bob Marley look-a-like being followed by a weaving pink penguin.

Seeing us heading towards the water sports hut, it was obvious they suspected some free entertainment might be in the offing - the medium-rare tourist with a hang-over trying to water ski. You could see folks adjusting their position to get a better view towards the sea.

I followed Bob Marley across one hundred yards of burning white sand to the boat, which was pulled just out of the water, tilting to one side. Not a bad looking boat, I thought, especially the bloody great Mercury outboard tilted up on the back. Looked like a fast ride.

Bob's clone was standing sullenly next to it with a hostile smirk on his face. This one reminded me of Eddie Grant and I got the impression he didn't like his customers very much. Maybe he was one of the buggers I had told to sod off earlier on?

Anyway, thirty dollars changed hands, with the promise of the change when we got back. To wake myself up, I flopped into the shallows, the water immediately cooling me down and making me feel marginally better.

I strode back out of the water with a little more purpose to don the offered life vest, which looked like it had been salvaged from a sunken wreck and was probably as much use for keeping me afloat as a tee-shirt. But it was obligatory.

In a voice which oozed "I don't give shit", Eddie started to give me some basic instructions, assuming I was a complete Muppet and had never water-skied before. I didn't mention I was an accomplished mono-skier from earlier days and decided to play the part of the hung-over English tourist.

The boat was pushed back into the water, and Eddie dropped the engine, which then burbled into life and he nudged the boat out of the shallows. I waded in, sat down in the water and put the two skis on. Making sure I was pointing in the same direction as the boat, I cleared the towrope and assumed the ready position in the water.

Thumbs up and Eddie rammed it. The back of the boat dropped, the engine roared and it shot forward, obviously on full power, which wasn't really necessary and can actually be quite dangerous. Shit-for-brains behind the wheel didn't care and was obviously trying to pull my arms out of their sockets.

Most of the beach was now watching the pink penguin who'd been asleep for hours and was half burnt to a crisp, who had stood up to immediately fall down, and had consumed pretty much an entire bottle of Mount Gay. Those who weren't aware of the preamble were simply bored on the beach and happy for some entertainment. It was obvious they were all sensing a disaster and hoped for a laugh.

As the rope became taught, I immediately rose vertically out of the water like Excalibur, stood up onto the two skis for a couple of seconds before kicking one of them off and side-slung out of the wake on mono-ski. The guys in the boat looked back, wide-eyed and amazed, but I know that the amazement was quickly replaced by annoyance that the pink penguin wasn't making a complete dick of himself and they might actually have to use some fuel.

Even though Eddie and Marley tried their best to shake me off, I managed to stay up the whole time, anticipating their every move, as they were no match for Spikey in Exmouth Estuary! I skied for exactly the allotted time and on the dot of the twenty minutes, Eddie turned the boat back to shore and I curved out to pick up speed to be able to ski right up to the sand next to the beaching boat without the tow-rope.

As I started to step out of the ski, I was sure I could hear applause from the beach. Seems like the audience had been entertained, but not in the way they had expected.

I shrugged out of the life vest and asked for my two dollars change.

"Dat's de tip, marn" Eddie sneered. I blinked.

"No, it's the change" I said. Eddie looked at me challengingly.

Now, if you've been skiing in any form whatsoever, water or snow, you'll know that if you've been going fast, your whole body will have been subjected to constant juddering, with your legs doing their best to act as shock-absorbers. Water skiing on the open sea is the worst. So, in my case, that was twenty minutes of severe hammering on open water as Eddie and Marley did their best to shake me off.

Also, twenty minutes of severe pounding plus a good dose of adrenalin has an interesting effect on a belly containing three beers, two pints of Coke, a bottle of

Mount Gay rum and a large seafood platter with extra prawns. And that interesting effect decided to manifest itself as soon as Eddie mentioned his intention to pocket my two dollars change. Maybe the annoyance caused by their little scam was the trigger.

I stood still, looking at them. I blinked once, twice and Eddie and Marley suddenly looked scared. My eyes opened wide, rolled upwards, and whoosh! Five pints of fizzy seafood broth exploded out of my mouth at high pressure, all over the boat, the skis, the engine, and Eddie and Marley.

Showing a complete lack of concern for an unwell punter, Eddie and Marley, each dripping in goo, went bananas. Pawing at the spew all over them, they started yelling in Barbadian every expletive known to marn, only just audible above the howls of laughter coming from the beach.

I think it was the sheer horror of the revolting spume dribbling down their faces and covering their kit that made Eddie and Marley push their boat back into the water, fire up the engine and speed off in search of a jet wash instead of attacking me.

With the beach in hysterics, I was unable to do anything but stand up to my waist in a soup of floating shrimps and Rum and Coke froth. The half-digested gunge floating on the surface immediately attracted a shoal of fish which went on a feeding frenzy churning up the water, so there I was, standing in one huge, natural jacuzzi, pieces of crab and prawn hanging off my chin. I don't know why, but I turned to the beach and bowed. A huge cheer went up accompanied by lots of applause.

I immediately felt better as a bloke came down the beach and said "For that show, Mate, have a cold beer!" Don't mind if I do!

Just to finish this one. I visited Nick/John the next day to get the "hamper" that I'd ordered, which he had ready and waiting. The day followed pretty much the same pattern as the day before, but without the Mount Gay.

At about the same time of day, I was awoken by a shaking.

"Eh maan, du wan' de.......arghhhhhh", immediate recognition and he quickly retreated down the beach. I was never bothered again.

Before leaving

After a few more largely uneventful, but incredibly relaxing days, I decided to head into Georgetown for the evening. It was a bustling place, with a mix of locals and tourists creating a vibrant atmosphere. I ate from street vendors, and generally chilled out, going from bar to bar. The last bar I remember had a large exhibition sized bottle of Mount Gay in the window. Not being one of those folks who ever learns, that's all I can remember of the evening.

I awoke the next morning in my bungalow with a hell of a hangover and Lucy. WTF?

Lucy was an extremely large, dark brown lady, age indeterminate, probably came in at around one hundred and twenty kilos, hairdo like one of the Jacksons, and lips that looked like a couple of pink pillows. I won't go into the details of what had happened, mainly because I can't remember them. Anyway, Lucy seemed to like me.

I'd made the age-old mistake of "bringin 'em back to my place". Should never do that. Always go to their's - then you can bugger off discreetly or quickly when you want out.

Not knowing how to get rid of large Lucy without offending and risking the consequences of a pissed-off hundred and twenty kilo Bajan, she stayed a few days. It became evident that Lucy, having allowed me to sample her ample delights, was now fully expecting to get married, have numerous children, and live happily ever after with yours-truly south of the Thames.

Still trying to work out how to get out if this, it got to the point where we just sat on the veranda, staring into space, without uttering a word. Trouble is, Lucy seemed happy with this.

Finally, I lied, "I'm going home tonight , Lucy, so I have to say goodbye. I'll leave you my address and we'll keep in contact. I'll take you home on the way to the airport." With that, a handful of small dollar bills managed to convince her into the Moke, and I asked her to show me where she lived.

After passing Georgetown, we soon disappeared into the deepest, darkest area of Barbados, right in the centre of the island.

Asphalt soon gave way to mud roads. Brick houses soon gave way to tin shacks. Lucy's house, and I use the term loosely, was not much more than a load of pallets covered in corrugated iron, rubbish lying all over the place, stray dogs, goats, and very dodgy looking neighbours.

The sight of a relatively small, pinkish-white me squashed next to the enormous black Lucy in a tilting Mini Moke was attracting the interest of some of those neighbours. Eddie and Marley looked saintly compared to some of these characters, and I decided I'd better get out of Denver as fast as possible.

Not wanting to stop, but with no hope of kicking Lucy out of the car, I pulled up, left the engine running, walked round to help her out, and started to walk with her towards the shack. At the last moment, I pecked her on the cheek and called over my shoulder "I'll write!" as I legged it back to the Moke, jumped in and shot off in a cloud of dust, leaving the wide-eyed Lucy to watch me go. It was only at this point that she realized that this was not to be a fond farewell and came waddling after me. But I was gone.

Bloody men - only after one thing!

Hoping that Lucy had bought my story of going straight to the airport, I kept the door locked that night, all lights off and hid the Moke a few blocks away. Fortunately, I was not disturbed.

Next morning, I bumped into the two Liverbirds on the beach - much more my cup of tea - and we all shared another bottle of rum. That night, we all got together at their hotel, and had a bloody good time, if you get my meaning!

I must admit I did feel sorry for Lucy. She was actually a good soul and no doubt looked forward to a life that most of us couldn't even imagine. And this was on an island marketed as paradise for the European and American tourist, to come a spend their big bills.

I've often wondered if there is a light brown little me running around Barbados, a natural water skier with a liking to Mount Gay.

Sixteen years later, accompanied by my French girlfriend Chantel, I returned to Barbados for a holiday. I wore a floppy hat and sunglasses just in case.

SARTH IFREEKUH

South Africa. This was actually quite a long escapade, the trip lasting a couple of months, during which I came the closest to becoming that squid.

The Rooivalk

Working for an exhibition company in the UK, we were always looking for new business.   Totally out of the blue, we got the chance to pitch for an exhibition/air show for the British army down at their Aviation Centre in Middle Wallop, Hampshire.

Surprising even ourselves, we got a contract for a South African firm. At that time, the British government was putting out tenders for their new attack helicopter - this was big stuff! Half a dozen or so companies around the world were in the running.   If you think the car industry moves lots of money, just have a look at defence budgets!

Anyway, one of the companies vying for the business was Valk Aviation out of Johannesburg. Their war-machine was an eight-ton attack helicopter, the Rooivalk, a real evil looking monster.   Valk dis-assembled two of them at their headquarters in Johannesburg, put them in a C130 Hercules aircraft and flew them, along with all the technicians and associated crew to a staging plant in Cambridge. Here, the helicopters were reassembled and flown down to Middle Wallop for the show.

Our job was to set up the stands, lighting, electrics, hospitality etc. and generally help out the customers, in this case Valk.

As has always been my personal motto, if you have a job to do, do it better than the customer expects and always go that extra yard. Folks seem to appreciate it.

Well, these South Africans certainly did, especially when it came to wanting local knowledge on the best pubs and the like! I honestly think they knew they were never going to get the contract, as it had probably already been decided.....ahem... politics you know! But these guys were party animals, mostly ex-military, on a ten day, all-expenses paid jolly to England and were going to milk it for all they could. Who wouldn't?

So, me and the Bokkers got on famously, pretty much every night after the show, dining and drinking copious amounts of alcohol together; I soon became accepted as part of their team....but always being the one with the poofy British accent.

There is another story about the nosey nosey game here, but that's for another day.

After five very heavy days, it came time for us to wrap up the show, and for the Valk boys to re-trace their steps back to Bloemfontein in central South Africa. As they were leaving, their PR Director, Mark, pulled me aside and said ""Jack, thit was a bladdy fintistic job you did, my boy. If you iver come to Sarth Ifrikuh, you cin be sure we'll return the hospitility! You keep in touch now, my boy, you 'ear?"

We said our goodbyes, and that was that.

Until twelve months later, when I was on a flight to Jan Smuts Airport, Johannesburg…with a kit bag, a wad of cash and high hopes.

I'd kept in touch with Mark now and then after the show and had let him know I was coming to visit his country. Over the phone he told me "ixcellent, Jack, I'll try and git a guy to meet you, but we're viry bizzy at the moment, so don't holt your brith."

After twelve months, I suspected that what he really meant was "No way, José!".

The cheapest deal I could find from London to Joburg was with Air Sudan, stopping at Karthoum. Long trip, but all other direct alternatives were extortionately priced. I also figured stopping in Karthoum might be interesting. I was wrong. It wasn't.

Also, as I've mentioned many times already, I suffer from an acute fear of flying in large, packed passenger jets. Didn't matter if the plane was brand-spanking new. However, this was Air Sudan, the plane was certainly large, most definitely packed and looked as if it hadn't had any maintenance in years. I was terrified.

So, there I was, off again at a boarding gate, looking out of the terminal window at the Air Sudan DC 10, more like a a DC 9-1/2 with lots of sticky tape, and observing the dish-dashed crowds of brown-skinned folks who were, unlike yours truly, eager to get aboard. I had downed as many beers as I could in the bar before boarding was called to try to settle my nerves. I was shaking like a leaf.

Eventually, after surviving the cattle-herd rush to board, and twenty minutes of jostling and sweating I found my seat, sat down, and for want of distraction, pulled out the flight information magazine. And guess what - it was a dry ship! No alcohol served!

Thirteen hours cramped in a cigar tube with two hundred souls without a drink! I was either going to go nuts or have a heart attack! As the engines started, I was sweating profusely and was pale as a ghost. I must have looked bad as the fellow in the seat next to me asked if I was alright? When I croaked my predicament, he reached under the seat in front and pulled out a bottle of Vodka, unscrewed the top and offered me a swig. The man was a saviour!

Arriving at Jan Smuts International Airport, completely exhausted after a sleepless, terrifying journey and three-quarters of a bottle of vodka, I shuffled off the plane and got in line in the "Foreigners" immigration queue. In front of me were four young English lads, apparently off touring around South Africa. We got chatting and it was plainly evident they weren't short of a bob or two (no doubt parents' money) as they told me of their hotel here, their next stop there, all pre-arranged.

Then they asked me what I was doing there? Remember, I probably looked like Desperate Dan, unshaven, and red-eyed. I told them that I was alone and had no particular plans and might do a bit of hunting. Their reaction was, "Are you crazy? South Africa is a dangerous place to be by yourself." I agreed with them, asked if they'd ever been to Slough on a Saturday night, and said I'd take my chances.

Baggage collected, mine being the usual single, well-travelled over-shoulder kit-bag, whilst the lads picked up their brand new, never-been-used high-end ruck-sacks, we all left the terminal building, they looking for their hotel bus, and me….not really looking anywhere.

However, as we exited the terminal, parked right in front of us was a gleaming, black stretch limousine with blacked-out windows. The driver glanced down at what was probably a photograph in his hand and came over to me and asked "Mr. Ballentyne?" He was the splitting image of the young driver Argyle in Diehard.

The penny dropped - Mark had come up trumps after all. By the look of the limo, maybe he had more influence than I realized.

"That's me", I said, and handed him my kit bag as he opened the rear passenger door.

The four English lads were watching everything. I looked at them, winked, made a pistol out of my right hand and pointed it at them as I eased myself into the dark cool innards of the car. The look on the lads' faces was a sight to behold. They probably thought I was a Soldier of Fortune.

I just caught ".... on his own, my ass!" as I closed the door.

Always nice to be met at an airport!

Vincent

I spent a week with Mark and his buddies. We cruised around the Johannesburg area, went to Sun City, visited several game lodges and saw sights and did things which your average tourist would never get to see or do. Africa under that privilege was absolutely unbelievable and I fell in love with it there and then. Oh dear, that feeling again... never want to go back to the UK!

Obviously quite well-off, using the company cars and benefits, Mark was at one a hard-drinking Bokker, a hard-nosed businessman and a true gentleman if needed. However, after a week of burning the candle at both ends as well as in the middle, it was obviously time to for me to move on and let him get back to work, so I went solo.

I rented a car with the intention of driving south through Kimberley, famous for the diamond mines - and heightened racial tension - and continuing on down to Port Elizabeth, with the idea of then taking the Garden Route, heading west along the southern coast to Cape Town.

Harking back to what the lads had said in the airport, South Africa was a pretty dangerous place in those days, especially for white folk in the poorer black areas, as black folks were pretty much prohibited from the white areas. Racial equality certainly hadn't arrived here.

High walls, electrified razor wire, enormous villas with swimming pools on manicured tree-lined avenues for the whites versus vast, broiling tin-shack townships with no running water or sewage and barely any electricity for the black polulation. It was shocking.

Nelson Mandela had only just been released from jail after 27 years' incarceration, and there were very strong racial tensions in the country. So, there was I, about to drive alone through 1200 kilometres of South African heartland, no GPS or mobile phone, just a folded map and some cash in my pocket.

I left the relative safety of inner-city Johannesburg and headed out through the dusty townships, passing the famous Soweto, scene of mass protests and police crackdowns in the seventies. The heat was stifling, even with the car windows open – the air conditioning just blew in warm air. It was hard to imagine what life must be like for the souls who live in the townships.

The further I left Johannesburg behind, the more open and sparse became the landscape, with fewer and fewer villages. Making the minimal amount of stops for fuel and water, after some five hours driving, I eventually arrived at Kimberley and checked into a reasonable looking motel on the outskirts. The armed guard at the gate gave me hope that the car would still be there the following morning. It was.

After a fitful night's sleep, another six hours behind the wheel got me to Port Elizabeth, where I checked into the City Lodge, one of a chain of motels all over South Africa.

After a twelve-hour sleep and several showers to get rid of the dust from all the orifices, I took the plunge, and stepped out to find a local bar for a bite and a beer. At this point, I'll mention that I've learnt never to judge a place until I've been there, same going for people. However, going out that night to the local bars opened my eyes to the situation in South Africa. Tension was high and ever-present.

I ended up drinking in a bar with a fellow dressed in scruffy bush gear called Vincent. This is one fellow who's name I have not changed in the book and I'll never forget his name or face till the day I die.

Vincent was an Afrikaaner, who are normally big, square headed bastards, but Vincent was a particularly small bugger. Small, but you wouldn't want to get on his wrong side. He looked like he could be a particularly nasty piece of work. Still, no worries, as we seemed to get on alright, drinking significant amounts of the local beers.

It got late, we'd had plenty to drink and the bar was getting ready to close. Then Vincent suggested that we go back to his place to continue drinking, and maybe do some fishing, as he lived next to a river. Well relaxed by the beers and Vincent's apparent friendliness, I thought like it seemed a great idea.

We went outside and got in his open-topped Wrangler jeep. Sitting in the passenger seat, I was on another planet, suffering from the effects of a 1200km drive, not too much sleep, several pints of Castle beer inside and staring at the stars through the scudding clouds lit by the moon. I seem to remember thinking it looked like rain, as the clouds seemed to be gathering.

After about twenty minutes driving, we stopped at a fuel station, middle of the night, middle of nowhere, as Vincent said he had to make a phone call. Strange. No re-fuelling, just a phone call? Then we were off again.

Now, I'm not sure if I have some kind of sixth sense, or no sense, but something suddenly made me stop enjoying the night sky. A feeling. Nothing more, but enough to start sobering me up. Now quite alert, we continued driving, when I noticed in the side mirror a second vehicle tag along behind, the headlights clouded in the dust from the back of the Jeep.

"Looks like we've got company" I said and turned to look at Vincent. He smiled coldly and said something which I don't remember, then pulled out a gun which I'll always remember. A big, shiny one which he then put to my left temple.

I blinked maybe once or twice and then, without even thinking about the speed at which we were travelling, I launched myself over the side of the Jeep's door. With a deafening bang, the bullet passed over my head missing me by a millimetre. I hit the asphalt at what must have been at least fifty miles an hour, rolling repeatedly. My Caterpillar boots took the brunt of the impact, shaving off all the steel clasps, but my legs came next.

I rolled over and down a slight bank and immediately staggered to my feet as the Jeep was screeching to a halt a few yards further up. I could sense the other car stopping further back as I careered off sideways into the darkness, hearing Vincent and his hyenas shouting and coming after me. Another shot sounded, but I just ran. The light was poor now, no moon or stars, but I heaved myself over what appeared to be a garden fence, conscious that certain death was closing in behind me. As I ran, it suddenly started to rain heavily

Barging through backyards, I banged on several doors, yelling like hell for help, but I guess, if someone bangs on your door at two o'clock in the morning in downtown Port Elizabeth, you don't answer.

I kept running, zigzagging and smashing through bushes, hedges, fences, washing lines, whatever I came up against. I don't know if it was the adrenalin or the survival skills picked up in Slough on a Saturday night, but finally, after what seemed like a terrifying hour or so, exhausted, bloody, bruised, completely out of breath, and soaked to the skin, I had to stop. I hid in a bush and listened. Nothing. There was no noise from behind and I figured I had lost my pursuers.

Looking at my watch, which had miraculously survived the impact, it was now 3am, pouring with rain. I was all busted up, my leg hurt like hell, I had a splitting headache and I had absolutely no idea where I was.

Plus, I had to assume there was a carload of bandits around somewhere looking for me. I limped onwards and eventually came to what must have been the same main road I had escaped from, now trying to think rationally as to how to get out of this mess. Fortunately, the rain started to ease, and a brilliant moon suddenly shone through a gap in the clouds – was this a sign from good ol' Saint Chris? "Is that you up there, Mate?" I thought to myself.

Then I heard a car engine and dived back off the road down the slope. Around the corner appeared a small car, which looked more and more like a white Fiat Uno as it got closer. Bandits don't drive clapped out Fiat Unos!

I scrambled up the slope and jumped into the middle of the road and literally stood in front of it, forcing it to stop by slamming both hands down on the bonnet. As you can imagine, the driver was petrified and I was lucky he wasn't armed as he would have surely shot me again, this time as a high-jacker.

The wide-eyed driver was a young black fellow. As the kid nervously got out, I slumped to the road in front of the car, the headlights shining on the blood.

"Hey man, are you ok?" he said, still shaken and very wary about what was going on, looking around like a startled animal.

Lying on the ground, between gasps, I quickly told him what had happened, showing him my bleeding leg and shredded clothing as evidence. He seemed to believe me. He was also smart enough to recognize the danger and said "We've gotta get outta here now, man". He helped me up and into the passenger seat and asked me where I was staying.

"The City Lodge."

"Wow man, that's way over the other side of the city!"

I had no idea how far it actually was, but after what seemed like an eternity, we eventually pulled into the City Lodge Motel. I told him to wait while I went to get some money for him, but he just said "Not a problem, but you take care now. South Africa is not a safe place for anybody right now, and the most dangerous are not the black people" and with that, he half-smiled and drove his little white Fiat off into the night.

I will leave you to guess his name. It started with a C.

The next day, I packed my gear, hobbled out to the car and, looking like I had been in a war zone, I left Port Elizabeth. If I could have met up with the young lads, they would have been even more convinced I was a Mercenary.

Thankful to be still in one-piece, next morning I drove off in my rental, heading south. The sun was shining, the brilliant blue sea was soon on my left, and feeling a lot better and grinning at myself for having survived yet another moment of madness, my Africa trip continued.

I followed the coast road, passing such places as Jeffries Bay, Oyster Bay and on to Storms River, the start of the Garden route, a three hundred kilometer stretch of coastline of outstanding beauty. Reaching Mossel Bay, I then left the coast and continued on to Stellenbosch and Cape Town, the jewel of South Africa.

It was awesome. I visited the vineyards of Stellenbosch and Zonnerbloom. I went to L'Agulhas, the most southerly point of the African continent (no, it is not the Cape of Good Hope which is further north) , and then headed on to Cape Town, to meet up with Spikey, my old water skiing buddy from Devon, whom I hadn't seen in twenty years. Remember him?

He hadn't changed, still a handsome git and doing very well for himself, as he always had.   He lived in Constantia, and that kind of says it all - the Mayfair of Cape Town. I spent about ten days there, partied too much, spent too much but soon got the feeling it was time to move on. Spikey was settled, had a well-paid job, money didn't seem to be an issue and he hadn't changed at all. Devil-may-care, life was just one big party.

I told him during yet another hangover I was moving on, but to where?   He suggested Mauritius by way of a relax before heading back to the humdrum of the UK. Apparently, there were some very good deals to be had from Cape Town.   Remember massed tourism was only just starting and Mauritius was still considerably under-developed compared to what it is today.

A day later, I was flying over the French island of Reunion to Mauritius, for a two-week full board beach holiday. There's not much more to say about this trip, apart from I remember two fellas staying at the hotel, Norbert from Holland, and Andy from America.

Both were on contract to service and repair high-speed weaving machines, as the textile industry was big business on the island at that time.   They would both go to work at six in the morning and be back in the bar by eleven. Plus, they got paid for it! As for me, two weeks full-board cost me three hundred pounds. You can put another zero on the end today.

The Victoria Falls

From Mauritius, I flew directly back to Johannesburg. Here, I met up with 'Ironknickers". Lynette was an 'Untouchable" promotion girl (ie. model) I'd worked with for many years in the old days of the motor exhibitions.   I'd tried for five years to unlock those ironknickers, but obviously my can opener wasn't sharp enough.   So, our relationship remained "as friends, let's keep in contact", which we did.

She was travelling with a guy who looked like an after-shave model, tall, muscular, and with a chin like a snow plough covered in iron filings. They invited me to join them for a few days. "Great" said I, wondering if I could do a Vincent on Mr. Old Spice.

Anyway, as time went by on the road trip, it became evident that even Old Spice's tin opener wasn't going to cut it, so to speak, and they also were just friends, and that was exactly what everyone would remain – just friends. I met up with Lynette many years later, but that's for another time.

We crossed into Zimbabwe, once known as the Jewel of Africa, heading north to Bulawayo. The country was ten years into Robert Mugabe's rule, and in those early days he was still courted by the international community and Zimbabwe was a lovely place. It would not always be like that.

We drove though stunning countryside, the people were friendly, and we stayed in some rustic hotels, game lodges and even some swanky colonial places. On this, I'll give you a tip. Never play squash with a guy who looks like he could handle a triathlon before breakfast, on a court with no air-conditioning when it's one hundred and ten degrees outside and you'd set the pace in demolishing half a case of Tormentoso Pinotage the night before.   Just in case you get the opportunity.

On we continued to our main destination - the Victoria Falls. Here we said our goodbyes, as Lynette and Old Spice had to get back to work, and they headed on to Harare.   I, on the other hand, checked into the Safari Lodge, a beautiful hotel built pretty much entirely of bamboo and which overlooked a watering hole which was visited by elephant, wildebeest and all sorts of other animals after sundown. It was awesome seeing these creatures come at sunset and throughout the night to drink.

Day one I spent exploring the Falls Nature Reserve, sitting on the edge of the cascade, lying in pools only a few feet from the edge of the thundering precipice and literally soaking in the might and power of that magical place. It was unbelievable, nature at its most magnificent.

It was at the Falls that I met Ingrid and Jan, an elderly Dutch couple who didn't seem to like each other very much. They were staying at the famous Victoria Falls Hotel, a very desirable establishment which I couldn't afford. We seemed to get on famously. Well, me and Ingrid did, and me and Jan did. Jan and Ingrid didn't. After the first evening, as I was about to leave, they invited me to a piano recital that was to be held the following night in their Hotel. How cool is that?

After a siesta in the Safari Lodge, I got as togged up as best as I could, i.e. a shirt with a collar, and slacks. On arrival at the Victoria Falls hotel, a large doorman blocked my progress and informed me very politely that Sir is required to wear a tie for the concert. You kidding, in the middle of Africa? Bugger! I told him that I had a set of jumper cables out in the car. If I tied them round my neck, would that do?

He said, "Ok, but I don't want you coming in and starting anything." (Sorry, had to get that one in!).

In actual fact, the hotel kindly lent me a hideous purple tie, straight from the 1960's, and in I went, looking like Sasha Distel. The guests probably thought there was a comic act before the concert.

It was everything I'd imagined. A grand main atrium full of overweight Westerners drinking gin and tonics, average age sixty, all in suits and tie's, the ladies in long dresses, and with several dozen immaculately dressed waiters keeping everyone well attended. I found Ingrid and Jan, along with six or seven others and they had left a space for me at their table. Yes, in between Ingrid and Jan of course. Another round of gin and tonics was sent for.

In the centre of the atrium were two grand pianos, back to back, looking like they'd be more at home in Vienna, but adding to the scene with absolute splendour and extravagance. The pianists entered and the concert began. It was awesome. The place, the atmosphere, the music. I felt as if I had been transported back in time to another era of opulence and privilege. For some.

Rafting the Zambezi

The following day, a little jaded, I decided to go white water rafting. On the Zambezi. Over two thousand four hundred kilometres long, the fourth largest river in Africa, the Zambezi is renowned to be one of the toughest rivers in the world to raft. Especially when you do most of it outside the bloody raft like I did.

There were about half a dozen of us in the raft, some South Africans and some Europeans, with the pilot/skipper, Hans, half-sitting, half-standing in the middle and steering with two bloody great oars. Our job, under his instruction, was to throw our weight around to keep the raft balanced going through the fast, deep rapids. So, wearing a life jacket and a variety of different coloured, plastic crash helmets which were more like cheap plastic colanders, we all piled in the boat which was stationary in the shallows. Most of the folks were joking and laughing, but not enough to hide the fact that there were some pretty anxious punters in the group.

Everyone clutching tightly on the grab-ropes, we push off into the wider river, the gentle current soon carrying us away from the bank and towards the middle of the flow. It wasn't long before the speed gradually picked up and as such, so did the breeze in our faces. Apart from a bit of nervous chatter, there was very little sound, until after only a few minutes, we could start to hear a distant roaring noise.

Looking forward anxiously, we could see what appeared to be the end of the river, with clouds of steam beyond. It seemed like the river was falling off a cliff. The roaring got louder and louder as we approached, picking up speed.

Since the off, Hans had been giving us instructions, and he now was having to raise his voice as the noise of the river increased. "Get ready, hold on tight and follow my INSTRUCTIONS!" The last word was pretty much drowned out as the roaring drowned him out and the raft accelerated to warp speed "Hold on tight?" No kidding!

The raft shot over the edge and plunged down a wall of water smashing into a great explosion of foam at the bottom. The bloke sitting in front of me lost his hold and flew back into me, knocking me clean out of the raft even though I was holding the grab line with both hands. I went into the maelstrom of foam and churning water, and after what seemed like an eternity came up next to the raft, but still managing to cling with one hand to the grab rope.

I was terrified I was going to get castrated on a bloody great rock under the water and with the sole intention of protecting the Ballentyne lineage, managed to haul myself from under the boat along the side. The raft was now hurtling towards the next wall of water, Hans was yelling at the top of his voice fighting with the oars and it was apparent that none of his crew had the faintest idea what to do, had no intention of following Han's instructions and simply hung on for dear life.

Meanwhile yours truly was doing a good impression of a fender lying parallel to one side of the raft, clinging on for dear life and going under water every two seconds. And there I stayed for about three miles, involuntarily drinking more Zambezi in twenty minutes than I had voluntarily slugged Pinotage during six hours in the bar.

The raft careened down the whitewater at what seemed like a hundred miles an hour, swinging this way and that, sometimes going half under water, then popping out at the near vertical, threatening to upend and dump everyone in the foam. Everyone was screaming and yelling, and no-one seemed to notice that the raft was one-person light. And that person was getting slowly drowned whilst keeping as best a look out as possible for rocks that threatened to smash him to pieces.

Only when we eventually reached a wide stretch of calm water where the trip was to end did they then notice my head bobbing in and out of view over one side. I was exhausted and my arms felt as if they had been pulled out of their sockets. However, the punters, realizing that they had survived, and it was over, were now gasping thankfully, looking back up the river and generally congratulating themselves. Hans looked down at me, still flopping in the shallows by the raft and said, "You like swimming, mate?"

To add insult to injury, with the raft out of the water, we were then supposed to climb out of the canyon, about a thousand feet up, soaking wet, exhausted, carrying the damn raft. As I had one arm about two feet longer than the other from three miles of white-water pounding, I stated emphatically "I didn't come down in the boat, so I ain't carrying it back up. Have a nice day!"

Back to Blighty.

The following day, I left the Zambezi, Zimbabwe and a thousand memories of mother nature. During the flight back, strangely enough I wasn't in the slightest bit bothered with the fear. It was an old plane, so old in fact I had to sit next to the rear gunner. Luckily, there were no bandits en route back to my old girlfriend, Joanna.

After a three day wait in the Garden Court Hotel, playing poker with the locals, I finally headed to the terminal building, feeling a little melancholy. Ah, but wait, I knew the return flight was going to be dry, so I spent two hours drinking Bloody Mary's in the terminal, chatting to anybody and everybody, even if they didn't want to chat. Yes, I was that guy.

As soon as the flight took off, I fell into a deep slumber, my body catching up after two months of abuse. But what two months! When the wheels hit the tarmac at Heathrow, I awoke, looking like some kind of road accident.

Ok, now where's my bag? The one with all my documents, passport, wallet, and most importantly, twenty rolls of priceless film (remember those?) As everyone disembarked, I asked the stewardess who said she had no idea where it was, as this crew had only come on board at Khartoum.

Now the aircraft was empty, apart from an army of cleaners preparing it for the return trip. I, along with the cabin crew, was searching everywhere, but no luck. Finally, I had to leave the plane, and walked to the terminal in a whole pile of trouble, to be met by a sour-faced immigration officer, who took me to a special holding room. Now what?

At that precise moment, a fellow in a fluorescent vest came barging in, brandishing my bag. "This yours, Mate?" I could have kissed him. One of the cleaners had found it buried in an overhead locker, under a load of life jackets. I can only assume that one of the original non-alcoholic crew had done it on purpose for getting on the plane accompanied by quite a few

Bloody Mary's.   The fact that I had slept from the moment I'd embarked, had gone unnoticed.

Footnote

It would be another twenty years before I returned to Africa, this time on my way to Namibia.

Africa has changed enormously in the last thirty years. Many things have happened, many countries have gone through all sorts of upheavals, some for the better, some for the worse. Nelson Mandela has come and gone, Robert Mugabe too. The continent is still ravaged and raped for its minerals and its diamonds. But one thing will never change - the magnificence of Mother Nature.

Go when you can.

OZ AND THE RUGBY WORLD CUP

This is one of my more recent escapades, me well into mid-life but with no more of a crisis than the previous thirty-nine years. Like South Africa, I'm going to have to be brief on this one as the adventure could fill several books.

I had always wanted to go to Australia, and the 2003 Rugby World Cup was too great an opportunity to miss, killing several birds with one stone. I had had some success with some properties back in the UK, had some money in my pocket so this was to be a slightly more lavish adventure than my usual escapades. So, here goes.

The opportunity of a lifetime

Having never had the remotest interest in football, I have always followed international rugby with a passion. This was rugby union, and this, as an Englishman, had the potential to be our finest hour. The 2003 Rugby World Cup to be held in arch-enemy territory - Australia - with the final in Sydney. A trip not to be missed.

I, like many, had a feeling that England had a very good chance of winning, even on Australian turf. I felt this for three reasons. Firstly, the major opposition teams, particularly the Southern hemisphere "Big Three" were not their usually well-oiled machines, still excellent, but not playing at their normal high standards. Secondly, our guys were running on all twelve cylinders, a brilliant, mature team with a top-class coach in Clive Woodward. And finally, it was to be for many of our players the last chance – international level retirement was looming; it was now or never, and they knew it.

I booked a package deal in the UK. Business class flights with Emirates, via Dubai, 5-star arrival accommodation in Perth, all the England group stage match tickets, and the quarters, semi's and the final. Cost me a small fortune.

The biggest issue however was that all the pool matches were to be played at different stadiums across Australia, and when you think that the distance from Perth to Brisbane is about 4500 kilometers, it a bloody big country. About the same sailing distance from the Canaries to Brazil in fact, should you ever be stupid enough to attempt such a feat!

Now, whereas most normal folks would fly from A to B, as you know, I was not normal. Plus, I had already shelled out close to twenty thousand Aussie dollars and not even left the UK yet! Still, I had a plan up my sleeve!

Departure was set for late September, and I couldn't wait. This was going to be a couple of months of high-octane adventure. In case you are wondering, yes, I was going on my own. Again.

An un-planned addition

About three weeks prior to leaving, I was invited to a party up in Chester. It was a great night, about forty people, quite a few of whom I knew from days gone by. In the early hours of the morning, everybody was pretty well shredded. You know the scene, smoke-filled room, slower music playing, people looking for the remaining dregs in the last few bottles, and the single guys looking for a hot water bottle to keep them warm that night.

I'd been talking to a girl called Jackie and the subject of Australia came up. Not exactly a supermodel, Jackie was most definitely getting higher up on the hotwaterbottleometer as the beers slid down.

I am not quite sure of the details, but at some point, I must have jokingly invited her to join me on a two-month epic journey across the Australian Outback. When will I ever learn not to have that one last bloody beer?

Anyway, the party ended, we all crashed out and I left fairly early the following morning for work with a thick head. I remember I didn't see Jackie as I left.

Fast forward a couple of weeks, the big day was approaching when I received an un-expected phone call.

"Hi, it's me, Jackie?"

"Err....Jackie, hello. How are you?" I stuttered, desperately trying to remember who the hell Jackie might be.

"Well, I've booked it! I'm going!" she excitedly announced down the phone.

I said "Great. Where are you going?" still wondering who Jackie was and what this has to do with me.

"AUSTRALIA! I arrive two days after you. I'll meet you in Perth on the 25th and we'll travel across to Sydney together just as you said!"

Holy shit!

Perth

The flight was wonderful, I think! I didn't know, even at my ripe old age of forty, that I could drink so much champagne, especially over eighteen hours of flying time with a stop-over in Dubai.   Neither did Emirates.

Anyway, a little pink around the gills, I arrived in Perth for the first major England game against South Africa. Emirates provided their courtesy transfer from the airport straight to The Crown Plaza Hotel which was in fact, right next to Perth's original airport which was now just a huge flat area of grass.

As it was very early, I was unable to check in to my room, so the receptionist, a stunning young Australian girl who's smile made me just so happy to be a guest, suggested I leave my luggage with the concierge and maybe take a stroll around the waterfront and sample Perth outdoors.

"Sounds like a plan" I replied, still besotted by her youth and beauty.

Conan the Bronzed Barbarian Doorman took away my bag, and the girl behind the desk continued (think in Australian accent now) "Right, let me just give you a little slippy!".

"Fantastic", I answered "I haven't had a little slippy for quite a while." looking at her with a dead pan face.

She paused, looked up, then blushed and smiled, before handing me a ticket. Over the next two days, I built up quite a rapport with Slippy such that on the second day, I was going to make my move and ask her out for a drink. I approached the desk, and there she was, with that same smile, looking quite frankly, ravishing. Just as I opened my mouth, a female voice screeched across the lobby.

"Yoo-hooo! Jack, it's me. I'm here!"

I tensed and Slippy looked at me with one of those feminine all-knowing looks, like she'd just been given a pardon from the electric chair. Chester Jackie ran over, and, quite literally, jumped off the floor and onto me.

"Holy Shit" I thought, again.

Fast-forwarding over the next twenty-four hours, the following night which was the night before the first England game against South Africa, and I sneaked out alone. I had a mission. The England team was billeted at The Hyatt, not far away.

I got to the hotel and walked straight into reception, which was heaving, but surprisingly there was no real security. The atmosphere was very pleasant and relaxed. I met quite a few of the England team, wishing them all good luck, and, as I expected, they were all very much well-behaved gentleman. It was Fort Twickenham in Australia, players mixing with fans. Imagine that in football? In fact, imagine that in today's highly professionalized rugby world? It's all changed.

Anyway, to keep it short, England v South Africa, pool game and England won. This first match produced a couple of events that will always stay in my mind.

Firstly, I met the Pope for the second time.   He was sitting a few rows down from me in the stadium, fully robed.   He had a staff, mitre, cloak, the works. Most importantly, because The Vatican wasn't playing, (they'd been knocked out by Diego Garcia in the preliminaries), he'd obviously chosen England as the team to support.

Secondly, I recall another guy on his own, wearing an England top. He was a diminutive chap, probably mid-fifties, completely dwarfed by eight huge, green-shirted South African's – Bokkers - that were sitting a couple of rows behind him.   They were massive, square heads, cropped cut blonde hair, drinking vast amounts of Heineken and chanting in Afrikaans, going ape-shit when their team looked like scoring, but blasting out every expletive known to man when we got points back or the referee blowed in England's favour.

By the final whistle, England had easily taken the game 25-6, and these gorillas sat down, utterly dejected and in total disbelief at what had just happened.   At this point, the little fellow from England stood up, slowly turned around, and quietly started singing, at the same time, pointing at the Bokkers.

"It's all gone quiet over there, and it's all gone quiet. It's all gone quiet, it's all gone quiet over there!"

He repeated it, this time much louder and with more passion, while still pointing at the disbelieving Bokkers who's expressions of surprise were quickly turning to anger. Talk about a red rag to a bull. I honestly thought they were going to leap over the seats and rip the fellow's head off. By now though, he had been joined by twenty thousand buddies so the Bokkers decided it was only a pool game, drank more beer and went back to being good-natured.

And yes, that's how many Englishmen went to Australia in 2003, with the same hunch I did.

Cocklebiddy and The Sheepshearers Inn

The following day, I hit the road with my two new companions. Jackie and a serious hangover, and I wasn't sure which one was bothering me more. My master plan was to travel thousands of miles of Australia without spending a fortune whilst allowing me to explore the mysteries of the great Aussie outback by…yes, you guessed it….a rented motor-home. Two months, unlimited mileage (thank God) and with the option of leaving it in Sydney.

Before we departed, we gave the van the once over. It certainly wasn't the spotless zero-kilometer example shown in the brochure, but looked and sounded solid enough, the engine ran sweetly and I was assured by the manager that the television worked, as there were dozens of games to watch during our tour.

We headed south out of Perth heading for the Margaret River, stopping in Freemantle, climbing the Gloucester Tree, then turning north by north east towards Cocklebiddy, the gateway to the great Nullarbor Plain and the east coast.

Up until now, there hadn't been any games to watch, so I hadn't tested the telly, but when we arrived in Cocklebiddy, there was another pool game that was worth watching. The home side, Australia, were playing.

Parking up in a lay-by just outside of town, out came the beers, and we settled down in the warm evening sunshine with the TV perched on a suitcase. However, it took only a few minutes until it became perfectly clear that there was no chance. We had power, absolutely no picture and kick-off was only ten minutes away. SHIIIIIIIIT!

Not thinking about the beers consumed, we jumped back into the van and sped into town, stopping at the first bar that looked promising. A wooden shack of a place, crappy sign swinging in the evening air, with some twenty dusty, beat-up pick-up trucks parked haphazardly out front.

Always one to err on the side of caution, and having seen a few Westerns in my time, I went in through a back door. The place was full of sheep shearers. Enormous blokes, averaging 150 kilos and all wearing hats. All had a beer in hand and lo and behold, they were all focused on the TV in the corner above the bar, watching the end of the national anthems. "Rock and roll" I thought. Seemed nice enough.

I sprinted out of the front door without being noticed and yelled to Jackie "We're in! Come on, it's just starting!" I then did something which was most definitely not on the side of caution. I pulled on my England shirt.

The two of us went back into the bar this time using the front entrance. Closing the door behind me, and possibly unaware of what I was about to do due to the excitement of the game, I announced as loudly as possible, in my best Queen's English

"Good evening Gents, are you chaps by any chance watching the Rugger?"

You can imagine the response.   They all turned in unison like a beast with twenty heads and forty evil eyes. There was silence as they tried to comprehend what this bleedin' Pommie was doing wearing an England shirt and coming into their bar with a Sheila in the middle of no-where during an Aussie game!

"Oops" I thought and swallowed, now realizing the folly of my enthusiasm.

The silence lasted for another fifteen seconds or so then the place exploded! "It's a bloody POM! Would'ya fuckin' believe it!   Gid over 'ere mate! Whaddaya drinkin' sport?"

Amazing! Incredible hospitality. Sheila – sorry, Jackie - quickly lost her ashen face and we both relaxed, feeling immediately at home. These were rugby men, and before we knew it, a space was made at the bar, and we settled down.

Now, I can't remember who was playing the Aussies, but obviously I was gunning for the opposition, which was a joke because I do remember it was a massacre. Such was the result that the sheepshearers were well and truly in party mood and the drinking and the banter really started. At this point, Jackie took her leave and escaped to the Camper fearing a bit of shearing might be at risk.

Once she'd gone, a big bloke next to me said, much to the delight of his mates, "We once heard a rumour here in Cricklebiddy, that you Poms could drink. Can't be true, can it?"

The evening progressed, the music got louder, some local Sheilas arrived, and dancing began, including on the pool table. I swapped my England top (I had two more) with a fella for his "Nice beaver" T shirt. I often wondered, after Australia lost the final, did he burn it or cherish it as a fond memory of a great tournament.

One by one, the Sheep Shearers left or passed out and who was the last man standing? The bloody Pom!

The Nullarbor Plain

The following morning, the three of us left Cocklebiddy - Me, Jackie and the hangover - and headed east, across the awesome Nullarbor Plain. Just over 1100 kilometers across, it boasts the longest straight sections of road on the planet which, every so often, act as a runway for the small planes to land. The road and the railway run parallel and service the sheep stations dotted along the route. It really is a vast expanse of nothingness and it took us two days to get across.

Then we hit the Great Ocean Road along the south coast of this fabulous country, visiting the Twelve Apostles, a collection of limestone stacks off the shore of the Port Campbell National Park in Victoria. Even though there were in reality only nine of these strange limestone pinnacles, some reaching 150 feet high, we couldn't know that in 2009 one would fall over, and that the sea would slowly and surely continue to erode the others away.

Looking south at the awesome scenery from the cliff tops, the next land mass would be Antarctica.

The next stop was Melbourne, and by pure coincidence, it was the weekend of the Melbourne Cup, the world-famous annual horse race which was part of the Melbourne Spring Racing Carnival. Sun, enormous crowds, booze and partying everywhere. We, however, having just driven almost 1500 kilometres in two days, just crashed out for the night at a nearby campsite.

Next day though, the Saturday, we got togged up and caught the bus to the racecourse. What a day that was! The drink flowed, the sun shone, we spoke to countless people, funnily enough, more about rugby than horse racing, and gambled. On that note, a personal thank you to Mr. Dettori for riding the last winner and injecting six hundred bucks into my coffers. A great day.

Mac and The Sydney Rugby Club

I'll skip forward now, a month into the tournament, and things were hotting up. Quite honestly, as this was fifteen years ago, I can't remember the precise chronological order of play, but a certain thing I'll never forget. The English fans were remarkable.

I met guys who had flown out just for a couple of weeks, expecting Dad's Army - the name the Aussies had given our team, as most were veterans - to be out of the competition by then. However, England stayed in the tournament and these English fans wound up extending their air-tickets as the white-shirted Army marched on relentless. Some were apparently putting their jobs at risk, racking up credit card bills, losing sweethearts and even wives.

Every game I went to, the Pope was there. He could always be spotted because of his mitre (that's' his Pope hat!) sticking up above the crowd. There was something else that demonstrated the strength of the English presence. We'd go to a game where England wasn't even playing, for example Ireland against Namibia, and after only a short while, the stadium would be resounding with "Swing Low Sweet Chariot". Even the players stopped in mid play, looking around the arena in bemusement.

Even though I am an England fan, this spirit is true of all rugby followers of all teams. Tremendous cameraderie, extremely entertaining and always wickedly friendly with the opposing team's supporters. Lots of good-humoured banter.

It was about then that a Glaswegian buddy of mine, Mac, flew out, as Scotland were still in the competition. Also, completely by surprise, another mate contacted me by email saying he was coming out for the final in Sydney as England had made the semis. He'd be flying all the way from Argentina!

Oh yes, and something else happened. Jackie jumped ship. She'd finally had enough of rugby, drinking, and fat blokes.   We parted company very amicably in Brisbane and promised to keep in touch, with her heading off towards the 'top end' of the continent and the Barrier Reef, and me driving the Camper back down to Sydney to meet Mac. I never did see her again.

Now in the company of Mac, a short, slightly over-weight Scot, far too bald for his thirty-two years, and most definitely lacking in the ways of foreign lands, we found a reasonably priced Camper Van site in the southern outskirts of the Sydney in a quiet suburban neighborhood called Sans Souci. The owner was a great guy called Bruce (no kidding). From the campsite we could get the train to downtown in about half an hour.

When I'd booked my trip back in the UK, the package included complimentary entrance tickets to the Sydney Rugby Club, presumably because I'd spent so much money.   This was to be VIP stuff, thought I.

We freshened up and headed off in search of the famous Rugby Club, both proudly wearing our respective teams' shirts. Mine was a made-for-the-tournament high quality England Rugby shirt, while Mac sported equally proudly, I must say, a faded old Scotland football shirt.   Mac wasn't one for airs and graces, but one of the nicest blokes you could meet.

We arrived downtown and headed to the Rugby Club, looking forward to watching the guys train and mingle with the players.   However, it didn't take long to realize things were not to be as expected. First suspicions arose as the address was very much "downtown". High-rise office blocks and shops. So urban in fact, that it was a stone's throw from the famous harbour. Hard to imagine a rugby field being there!

After to-ing and fro-ing for an hour or so, and asking a bunch of clueless people, we eventually found The Sydney Rugby Club. A seedy little rugby bar down a grubby back street, full of fat blokes wearing rugby shirts from all over the world. The walls covered in framed photographs of famous rugby moments and famous rugby players, everyone being extremely noisy, extremely friendly and drinking enormous amounts of Victoria Bitter. Not what we expected at all, but it was a great place!

As the days went by, The Sydney Rugby Club became our second home. Packed with memorabilia, with more and more fans arriving each day. English, Scots, Welsh, Irish, French, Kiwi's, Bokkers, Aussies, all taking the piss out of each other, then buying everyone a round. Simply a wonderful atmosphere.

We'd wake up in the motor home, take the train into town, eat lunch overlooking the harbour and the Sydney Opera house, then mooch on up to the Club. Unfortunately for Mac, Scotland was knocked out shortly after that, but he was having a ball. Being the only blue Scotland shirt left in the place he was constantly being commiserated by people topping up his beer! This was his idea of heaven, and he had another three weeks of it!

A few days later, Jim arrived from Argentina and our little group was now three - The Three Amigos.

Les Bleus

The Rugby World Cup final was now only a few days away. Dad's Army was marching on, sixty thousand white-shirted warriors, blessed by the Pope. The previous day and to our delight, the French team had been knocked out in their semi-final match.

We, meanwhile, maintained our routine of drinking in the Rugby Club from midday until darkness fell.   On this particular night and in celebration of the French demise, we decided to check out a few other bars and ventured out into the Sydney night.

One particular place soon caught our attention due to the TV vans outside, so in we went.   It was a much higher class, trendy nightspot than the Rugby Club. The joint was full of women, ratio of girls to blokes must have been five to one, easy. So, what's the deal here, we wondered, as we made our way to the UV lit bar to get a drink. Shouting across to the barman, he told us the French team had booked the VIP section to have a final blow-out before their departure back to Paris. Looking at the number of girls in the place, you'd think The Beatles were coming.

Anyway, the intel was correct. Les Bleus arrived, thirty or so huge fellas, all in suits and ties, all looking like cologne models and the girls went bananas.   In one way we were fortunate that we had arrived early because, by now, the doormen were barring any further entries.   However, we were unfortunate another way in that none of us we were six foot, nor did we speak with a French accent nor were we elegantly dressed in blazer and tie and nor were being interviewed and photographed by the local and international paparazzi. C'est la vie you little Ros Bief!

Now, here's the shitty part. Mac had arranged to meet some of his mates from Scotland at some place which was way across the harbour, so we had to leave. Jim and I were in promising conversation with two beautiful girls (and yes, this was without the enhancing effect of beer goggles) both of whom seemed to be enjoying our English accents.

In hindsight, we should have suggested to Mac that he went on his own, but of course we didn't, and the three of us left in total solidarity. An hour's trek over to the other side of the city, of course Mac's mates nowhere to be seen, so we trudged back in the early hours to the club. And no, we couldn't get back in. So, the three sad bastards took a cab in total disappointment back to the camper van. "Salop!" as the French would say.

The Final

22nd November was final night, the home team against Dad's Army. There was an unbelievable atmosphere in Sydney, and it semmed every single person was dressed in gold or white.

Mac didn't have a ticket, and being a Scotsman didn't fancy paying a fortune for one of the few being touted, so he ensconced himself in front of the biggest TV in the Rugby Club, now a VIP in his own right - all the staff loved him.

Jim and I were in the stadium and the atmosphere was electric. An hour to go, the terraces were packed, the music blaring, the beer flowing, the cameradie and banter between the Poms and the Aussies relentless but as always, good humored. Oh yes, and the rain was sheeting down as it had been all day.

There of course was the Pope, accompanied a few rows away by The Queen, over there was Richard the Lionheart and countless Crusaders, with Winston Churchill up behind us. All very happy to have their photographs taken with anyone who wanted, whatever shirt you were wearing, especially the Aussies.

Suddenly, I heard my name being shouted across the crowd, and I turned, completely mystified looking for the source. The call came again. Then, from behind a staircase, appeared Bill, an old friend from Kent University. I hadn't seen him for almost twenty years. Incredible coincidence - talk about a small world! Even the Queen was impressed! I didn't think that the occasion could have been bettered in any way, but that meeting with my old friend completely iced the cake.

I don't need to tell you about that game, but as sporting nail biters go, it was the ultimate. Mr. Wilkinson met Mr.Ellis, a last minute drop-goal and sixty thousand Englishmen went quite literally, bonkers. The Wizard of Oz had a new meaning.

I don't know how long it was after the final whistle when we reluctantly left the ground, exhausted after the tension of the match, but fuelled on elation and vast amounts of Four-X. Well-organised trains took the fans back into Sydney centre, Dad's Army now in excess of a hundred thousand.

We battled our way to the Rugby Club and found Mac in pole position, hosting the crowd. He was actually celebrating on our behalf, something that is never done by a Scotsman. The three of us then pub-crawled around Sydney in the pouring rain, getting soaked but oblivious to the cold, and every bar that was still open crammed to overflowing with white shirts and gold shirts. It was a fantastic atmosphere. More so if you were wearing a white shirt!

As usual, a few special things stick in my mind.

Firstly, the sportsmanship of the Australians. Every few minutes, a guy in an Oz top would stop, shake our hands, and say, "Bloody great game Mate. Best team won, good on ya."

Secondly, as we strolled down near the waterfront, probably about three in the morning, we bumped into Martin Johnson, the England captain, who just a few hours ago, had been watched by over half a billion people globally, lift the trophy. We all shook hands and moved on. Further on down we met a few more of the England players. It wasn't necessary to say much - the job had been done by all parties.

Lastly, I read a report in the press the following day that in Sydney that night, the police had made just one arrest; a guy had fallen over and dented someone's car with his chin. I'll say it again. That's rugby, and the great people who play and follow, it.

Hanging Rock

Jim had a day to spare before heading back to Buenos Aires. We'd heard about a place up in the Blue Mountains, a bit remote for the average tourist and which sounded just my cup of tea. We took the camper van and after driving north out of the city for a few hours, we eventually stopped at a Tourist Information kiosk for directions.

"Oh, you mean Hanging Rock" the lady said. "It's a place that's supposedly off limits to tourists, because it's too dangerous, but between you and me, if you take the road out of town heading north for three miles, turn down a track on the right that has a gate, park, and walk about a mile, you'll find it."

We followed her directions. We parked up on the edge of the asphalt road and started out on foot along a dirt track. We walked what seemed miles through thick scrub in thirty-five degrees heat, not really sure if we were in the right place.

On several occasions, Mac and Jim wanted to head back but I persuaded them to keep going, which they begrudgingly did. The heat was fierce, our water supply was getting low but on we trudged. The conversation had long finished.

Suddenly, after what must have been a couple of hours of trekking, the trees began to thin out to the occasional bush, and we nearly walked over the edge. A sheer vertical drop, two thousand feet down!

There were no barriers, no signs, nothing. Just a dust track leading to a rocky precipice and stunning view across the Blue Mountains. We could see for maybe forty miles.

Not to be confused with the more famous Hanging Rock close to Melbourne, this sandstone outcrop, well off the beaten track was a base jumper's paradise and was magnificent.

Jim surprised us all by producing a bottle of wine from his knapsack and with three plastic glasses we made a toast. To finding Hanging Rock, to friends and to Johnny Wilkinson.

The next day, back in Sydney and with the World Cup over, Jim left back to South America and Mac and I looked at each other with some time to kill.

The Great Barrier Reef

We returned the Camper to the rental company in Sydney. No surprises at all, deposit repaid, all good. A cab took us to the airport where we caught a flight up to Cairns. We were off to the Great Barrier Reef, something I'd dreamed of since, well, I could dream!

Our destination was Green Island, some twenty miles off the mainland, in the heart of the Barrier reef marine park. There were basically two ways of getting there, and, as with everything, the cheap way, a slow boat packed with two hundred tourists, or the expensive way, a six-seater seaplane that took thirty minutes.

As the Camper deposit had been returned without any deductions, we decided that two hundred tourists on a slow boat wasn't for us, so we were soon looking forward to meeting our four flight companions. Curious, but I never think of myself as a tourist!

The seaplane was at least thirty years old but was immaculate. A single engine job, with two impeccably dressed pilots and six passengers - Mac, myself and four Japanese tourists. Bobbing by the side of the jetty, the plane gleamed on its two enormous floats, with the water below so clear and turquoise it was almost unreal. The plane seemed to be floating in mid-air.

All of us safely installed and buckled up, the Captain cranked up the engine, which spluttered to life in a second. Giving a thumbs-up to cast off, the engine increased in volume and the plane nosed out towards the open sea.

Flaps partially down, the pilot opened the throttles, and with an almighty roar the plane gathered speed, the floats hunkered down, smashing through the swell, spray everywhere and water seeping into the aircraft through the door and roof. After what seemed like an age of buffeting and bedlam, the pilot suddenly throttled back and the plane sank back into the swell. "Too rough" he shouted back to his passengers.

The six of us just sat there without saying anything. The Japanese looked at one another, decidedly worried. Mac was crapping himself, whilst yours truly, the bloke with the fear of flying, was loving it. The tension eased and the Japanese started babbling to each other as only Asians can do.

After ten minutes of rocking back and forth, the pilot decided to have another go. This shut the Japanese up immediately. The engine roared again, and we were off, shooting across the waves, the buffeting so strong it seemed as if the plane would disintegrate. However, as the speed increased, the buffeting decreased and finally we rose above the ocean, instantly becoming a different creature, a free bird, at home in the sky.

Even though the cabin was extremely noisy inside, the smoothness of flight seemed so quiet compared to the buffeting we had just endured.

The higher we climbed, the engine provided a constant drumming as a soundtrack, the sea below became more and more translucent, an awesome turquoise carpet stretching to the horizon. We could see the corals, interspersed with gleaming white sand beds, fish, sharks and rays. Every now and then a flock of seabirds would fly below us just above the surface of the water. No one spoke. It was simply spellbinding.

I guessed we were flying at about two to three thousand feet, passing over the ferry that would arrive at Green Island two hours after us.   We could see for miles, dozens of islands, the Great Barrier Reef just a few feet below the crystal-clear water's surface, the shadows of the odd puffy, white cloud painting darker shapes on the sea below. Absolutely spectacular.

After far too short a time, the plane began to descend and serenely settled into the sea close to what must be Green Island. The six of us climbed out into a tiny rib moored to one of the plane's pontoons and we were taken to a small resort for breakfast. It was deserted. It was quiet. It was warm. It was deep greens and turquoise blues. Even the Japanese were silenced by the sheer serenity and un-touched beauty of the island.

I just couldn't wait to get into the water, especially keen to beat the two hundred odd tourists heading our way. I grabbed a pair of flippers, a mask and snorkel and in I plunged.

It was indescribably beautiful, just floating over the coral, absorbing the colours, in crystal clear water. Then, a couple of feet below me, a turtle appeared. Without any hesitation, I held my breath and dived down, grabbing onto its shell.

It didn't flinch, and as carefree as ever, just pulled me along for about twenty feet, until I had to surface for air. Being the animal lover that I am, it was magical.

After what must have been a good hour in the water, I decided to end the dream and headed back to the shore. I found Mac sitting on the beach drinking a beer with a fat American. God know's where he had come from.

Mac couldn't swim and had been happy enough to watch from the shore. I felt sorry for him that he was going to miss out on such a wonderful spectacle, but no amount of persuading would get him into the water. The dangers of being eaten by a shark were explained in full, no-nonsense, Glaswegian. "No fookun wee, Mate!"

Then the ferry boat arrived, and the world and his wife got off. The tranquil island was suddenly transformed into a mass of camera strapped, bright shirted, extremely loud tourists from all over the globe. Time to leave. We were back in Cairns for lunch.

The Indian Pacific Railway

Two days later, we were back in Sydney. Mac was leaving to go back to England and the treadmill in Chester. Perhaps it was the need for familiarity after the departure of my companions, so I headed back alone to Sans Souci. The beach looked out across the water to Sydney International Airport way in the distance. I could see the planes taking off, many turning as they climbed to a flightpath which took them directly overhead.

I sat there for a while, once again feeling very alone. In a moment of inspiration, I leapt to my feet and wrote in the sand, in letters twenty feet high, "Swing low, Mac!"

My flight back to Blighty was leaving from Perth in five days. Hmmm, wasn't that where Slippy was?

However, there was the minor issue of me still being in Sydney with the coffers running low. So, how to get back? Only one thing for it, The Indian Pacific railway!

It was a three-day train journey, east coast to west coast, going directly through familiar territory, my old friend the Nullarbor. It was marvellous! A restaurant car, a bar, my own berth, and a bunch of people who all had a story to tell, apart from myself of course, who had nothing to say. (Wink!)

Now, to say my berth was small is an understatement. Reckon if I had put the key in the door slightly too far, I would have broken the outside window! Nonetheless, the cabin had all the facilities, and it was my home for the next three days.

The trip was uneventful in that the train just kept on going, stopping occasionally in remote townships in the middle of nowhere. The last night before reaching Perth, I got talking to a young lady in the bar, who, for some bizarre reason, decided to spend the night in my cabin. Needless to say that we were both just a little bit tipsy.

As the train pulled into Perth Central next morning, I woke up alone, but on the floor next to my bunk was a ring, together with a single sandal. "How very odd" I thought. Well, I thought, I'm sure to find her on the platform to return her belongings. I never saw her again.

I was now back in The Perth Crown Plaza, after two months, fourteen thousand kilometers, and a further five thousand Aussie dollars out of pocket.

Slippy wasn't there. She had probably been pre-warned that the mad Englishman was returning and moved to Sydney. After a very pensive few days wandering around the city, I headed to the airport, and back home to the UK, not knowing what to expect on my arrival, but counting on work, rain, and traffic jams.

Meeting the Pope again!

To finish, one more anecdote. I was sitting in Business Class sipping champagne on the flight back, a thousand thoughts running through my head. To stretch my legs, I decided to take a stroll down the aisle to the back of the plane. As I parted the curtains into Economy, what did I see? A mitre sticking up from a row towards the back!

"Bloody hell, it's the Pope!"

I quickly went back to the Business Class cabin, grabbed a stewardess and asked for a bottle of champagne. She informed me that she couldn't serve a full bottle, but after explaining my reason for asking, she was eventually yielded. I walked back into Economy, bottle in hand, and approached the Pope. As he looked up to see who was bothering him, all I said was

"Swing low fella – I was three rows behind you!", and we enjoyed the bottle together.

It turned out, that before the World Cup, he'd lost a bet and his forfeit was that he had to go to every England game dressed as well, you know who.

Postscript to this story

Of all the people I'd met on the Oz trip, the one person I really wanted to, I hadn't. To commemorate the Rugby World Cup, I had a calendar printed, twelve of the best photographs, in sepia, all of very special moments. I treasure it to this day in my photo portfolio. Gold dust.

In 2015, twelve years after the tournament, I was in the UK when I saw an advertisement in The Daily Telegraph. There was to be a gala fundraising dinner in aid of the NSPCC to be held at The Grosvenor

House Hotel in Mayfair, and one of ambassadors of the charity was to be there.

I called my good friend Angus, and old boy of some eighty years but who liked these sorts of things. We managed to get two tickets, not at all cheap, but it didn't matter.

Now Angus had spent most of his career working as a civil servant in Africa and consequently he was a member of the Civil Service Club in London, and rooms were available.

It was an exceptional night. After all the formalities of the gala black-tie dinner and the speeches, I seized the opportunity, grabbed my calendar which I had carefully looked after all these years, and jostled my way to the front of the main hall. And there he was.

"Hello Johnny. Would you mind signing this for me?" whilst shaking his hand vigorously.

"Err…sure. What is it?"

As he flicked through the photos, it became very apparent to him what is was. He took his time, looking at each picture. He seemed to be almost disappearing down a time tunnel.

He looked up and gave me a huge grin and signed it with a note. We shook hands again, and that was that.

I don't suppose grown men should have hero's, but I'd finally met Johnny Wilkinson, who had kicked what was for me the greatest drop goal in the history of rugby union.

MR. RUTINI

If there's one place on God's earth that everyone should visit once in their lives, it's the Iguazu Falls in South America. Located on the borders of Brazil, Argentina and Paraguay, the Paraná river flows down from central Brazil to join the Iguazu river, which flows East to West from Southern Brazil. Just before they meet, the falls on the Iguazú river provides one of nature's true spectacles.

I was in Buenos Aires visiting my brother who was working out there when our Father (who wasn't in heaven) flew out for a week's vacation. Along with the golf, the Tango, and the Asados (Argentine Barbeques), on the agenda was a trip to the Iguazu Falls which none of us had visited before, but of which we'd heard many tales of beauty and magnificence.

The three of us caught a flight from Aeroparque, the domestic airport in Buenos Aires. The airport is on the southern bank of the enormous brown expanse of the River Plate, which is the confluence of the Uruguay River and the same Parana river that comes down from Iguazu.

As usual, my phobia of flying was kicking in because the usual calming session in the bar prior to departure hadn't happened; we were running late due to the rush-hour traffic. So, white knuckled and sweating like a pig, I endured the two-hour flight, which to make matters worse was packed to the gunnels and as bumpy as hell.

No surprises, we landed safely an hour later, dropping down towards the lush green fields and forest outside the town of Foz de Iguazú. A short taxi ride took us to the hotel which was much bigger and modern that we had expected, offering a pool, a couple of restaurants and a casino.

Now, the Rutini bit. Argentina is a major wine producer and has in the last twenty years really grown in exports. Argentine reds are certainly their forte, with the main grape varieties being the Cabernet Sauvignon, the Merlot and the Malbec. My favourite was certainly the Malbec, and one of the famous producers was the Rutini vineyard, or Bodega as they call it in Spanish.

So, we'd just arrived at the Hotel, Bro and myself were dressed in chinos, beige jackets, white shirts, Rayban aviator Sunglasses, both looking very similar and equally dapper, if I do say so myself. Our Father, (who still wasn't in heaven) was equally dapper, and being an ex-military man, had the usual dark jacket, slicked back hair, shiny shoes and authoritative demeanour. He however, didn't sport the mirrored sunglasses - his were the 1960's back rimmed ones. Remember Onassis? Kennedy?

As we often walked respectfully behind Dad, and he was always marching forward to get things done, he said, "Keep up. You two look like a couple of bloody bodyguards".

And that gave us an idea to have some fun. We entered the lobby of the hotel, my brother and I walking a few feet behind "Mister Rutini".

Bro stepped forward, approached the reception desk, and said, in fluent Spanish but accented to try to sound Italian, talking like his tonsils had been rasped by a wire brush.

"'ello. Reservation. Ballentyne. Two Rooms. Zis is Mr.Rutini. You kno oo ee iz? " and promptly stepped back behind Dad.

By the look on the receptionist's face, she wanted to say "Nope, do they make buttons?" But what she actually said was, "Err…Of course, Sir", while glancing to her superior in the side office. The Manager, a fellow in his fifties, shot out, straightening his tie whilst looking flustered but doing his best to be imperious. An immediate, greasy and entirely false smile spread across his face.

Even though Mr. Mealy was speaking Spanish, the gist of it was "Ahhh Señor Rutini, this is indeed an honour. We had no idea that it was you, due to the name on the reservation. Oh Dear, I see you are in a standard room. That cannot do!".

He turned to the receptionist and barked an order "Upgrade Señor Rutini immediately to the Deluxe Suite!" and turning back to Mr. Rutini, announced that "The upgrade to the deluxe suite will be at no charge of course".

Mr. Rutini – Dad - obviously hadn't said a word from behind his dark glasses as he had no idea what was going on as it was all in Spanish so he just nodded and grunted "Good".

Evidently the Manager was too busy kow-towing to notice or question why Mr. Rutini spoke English.

With Dad showing no emotion whatsoever, and with Bro and myself panning the lobby area in true secret service fashion that would have made the FBI proud, we walked towards the lifts, desperately trying not to burst into guffaws. The die was cast.

Some mafia boss who might or might not have something to do with one of the major wine producers in Argentina and his two minders were in town. We got to one of our rooms, opened the mini bar, and burst out laughing.

This act or pretence continued for the duration of our stay, Dad being treated like a gangster, the two of us always remaining a few metres behind him. It was absolutely incredible by keeping up this act what a difference in treatment we got. And not just in the hotel.

The following day, we made for the Falls. It was a short limousine ride – Mr Rutini doesn't take taxis. In fact, it was just a normal taxi but painted black with blacked out windows to give a dramatic impression. From there you take a narrow-gauge, open-sided train through the rainforest, continuing for a mile or so and finally arriving at a tiny station not too far from the cascade itself. The Mr. Rutini routine was now starting to get a bit silly, but what the hell, we were having fun.

The train was made up of maybe half a dozen open carriages. We, as Mr.Rutini's minders, ensured that the Boss was safely on the train, sitting alone at the far back end. Even though we didn't try to prohibit anyone else getting on our carriage, and all the others were packed, no-one else boarded our carriage.

The sight of two close-cropped, mean-looking gringos in shades, and an even meaner looking Godfather had persuaded the other tourists they'd better use the other carriages. As the train pulled out, there were five cars packed with people and one car with three dudes in it - Mr. Rutini and his two bananas.

The train stopped after a ten-minute rumble through dense forest, and you could now hear a faint roaring sound. There was also the smell of water in the air. The expectancy level was high and made us completely forget the Mr. Rutini act and we became three normal Falls visitors. And what a visit it was!

It was breath-taking. The Victoria Falls were awesome, but somehow the power and proximity of these falls were, well, quite frankly emotional.

A wooden, half-mile long walkway on stilts had been constructed that led over the head-water river right to the edge of the drop, enabling you to actually stand over millions of tons of water plummeting down hundreds of feet into the basin below. La Garganta del Diablo, or Devil's Throat.

The noise, spray and vibration were overwhelming, and we were drenched within seconds. After spending half an hour at the top and taking thousands of photos, marvelling at the sheer power and volume of water, we retraced our steps then took the hike down to the base of the falls. There, we boarded a semi-rigid inflatable boat, storing all our possessions in black plastic bin-liners, and once loaded, the boat charged right up to the base of the falls, as close as possible without being overwhelmed by the ferocity of the thundering water. It was exhilarating beyond belief.

Completely drenched, I felt once again totally together with Mother Nature, soaked to the skin, warm and cold at the same time, the boat rocking and heaving, desperate to get away from the maelstrom. The wind caused by the thundering wall of water was incredible. It was wonderful beyond words.

Half an hour later, we disembarked from the boat, and walked back to the train. There were toucans, parrots, and many varieties of exotic fauna in the park. It is truly a paradise that I pray never gets over over-commercialised.

The following day, we checked out, laughing and joking in English, which created some curious stares from the reception staff, and flew back to Buenos Aires, all three of us better human beings after experiencing that marvellous place (and the free Deluxe Suite).

On the last night of our visit, we went to a cracking steak restaurant, and ordered a seventy-dollar bottle of..........guess what? Yup. Rutini Cabernet-Malbec. Fantastic.

THE POND

How on earth did I get into this?

I've always liked like water. Not to drink obviously, there are far better options for that, but to look at, to be near, to hear, be on, or in. Especially if it's warmer than 25 degrees C and deep turquoise blue.

My early days, as you've read, were spent close to the sea and maybe that's where the love affair started. It is also my firm intention that my final chapters of life will be spent somewhere with a blue view.

Every love affair has its ups and downs, and this particular adventure provided extreme ups and downs every ten seconds.

So, to the story.

I was on a little sailing boat, mid-Atlantic, somewhere close to the equator, hoping not to be swallowed by the mountainous seas.

I'd seen enough bloody water to last a lifetime. I had five kilometers of the stuff underneath me, two thousand kilometers of it behind me and another two thousand in front of me, it was coming down from the sky in torrents to be then driven horizontally directly into my face by the howling wind. I swear saltwater was coming out of my skin.

The background to this adventure started in Greece, where I'd been living for the previous six months with the idea of moving to the sun and starting a laid-back business, living out a life of Mediterranean bliss, dark-haired beauties, moussaka and ouzo.

I suppose I should have gotten the hint that all wasn't to be as expected after the drive from the UK down through such places as Bosnia and Albania. The tourist brochures tell you they are wonderful places to visit, but when you aren't a tourist and go where the tourists don't go, it ain't funny. In fact, it was often downright frightening. Basically, you don't want to do that drive, but that's another story to be told.

So, to Greece itself. Bloody shambles of a country, unless you are Greek ,of course. It's also not warm and rains a hell of a lot in winter. And that's before it snows, when it really does get absolutely freezing.

The Greek experience was a story unto itself, but I'll simply mention it by way of an introduction into this chapter. Suffice to say I'd been in the country only a couple of months or so and had already invested in a tool-hire business venture with a Greek fellow.

This latest foray into entrepreneurship started with a week or two of enthusiasm and quickly went ..errr.. Greek! Lazy, local customs, confusion, no commitment, not serious. No chance of it bearing any fruit. And no, I couldn't speak any Greek beyond ordering a beer.

I know what you're thinking, and you're right. Daft. It was.

So, there was I, fortunately not having invested too much time or money, but completely convinced that Greece is for Greeks only, perhaps tourists on organized package deals but most definitely no-one else. The experience also underlined why, in my humble opinion, the European Union has a sorry future if this was an example of one of its main members.

Anyway, I gave it a go, it didn't work, and it was time to move on.

Hendrick and Ginny

I had been living right next to a yachting marina with many an hour spent sharing beers and trading stories with the yachtsmen and crews passing through. So it was that I met this South African couple who had flown up from Cape Town to the Mediterranean for the sole purpose of buying a boat and sailing it back home. Apparently, it would be cheaper. Not sure I agreed, but they seemed genuine enough.

There was immediate chemistry between myself and Hendrik, as I had plenty of stories to tell, including some from his homeland, and we both liked drinking beer. His wife was called Ginny. I suspect it was actually Jenny, but they pronounced it Ginny and I thought it was an enitely appropriate name having a hubby called Hendrick.

266

Ginny was cut from a completely different cloth to me, and I also think hubby Hendrick, and as the story unfolds, you'll see what I mean.

So, lots of beers over several days and a plan was hatched. Hendrick and Ginny would sail their recently acquired pride and joy "Big Bird", a tired, thirty-nine foot Dufour (which stupidly I didn't go and check out first) down through the Med to the Canaries, where I would hook up with them to help them across the pond to Brazil.

The geographically astute reader will ask why they didn't go down through the Suez Canal and the East Coast of Africa?

"Py-ruts, my boy!" said Hendrick, with a knowledgeable wink.

Ah yes, Pirates! Somalia is not a place to sail past these days.

I'll now fast-forward to the Canaries, as my trip back to the UK via Italy on an over-loaded rust-bucket car ferry to avoid the Albanian hit squads is yet another tale to be told. In fact, that bloody excuse for a ferry made the news a few years later because it caught fire and sank, an occurrence on which I should have betted heavily as it was obviously this was bound to happen.

So, after a week or so back in the UK to get as prepared as I could in such a short time, I flew to Tenerife on a one-way ticket with two hundred one-week package tourists. The few people I spoke to basically looked at me gob smacked when I told them I was on a one-way ticket as I was going to sail a small yacht across to Brazil.

Tenerife and The Perkins

I met up with Hendrick and Ginny at the Amarilla Marina on the south coast of Tenerife. Expecting to find the happy couple relaxed and ginning-and-tonicking with the best of them, it seems that the old adage of "you get what you pay for" well and truly applied to Big Bird. It seems they had had pretty severe weather all the way from Greece and Big Bird had leaked like a sieve.

Having been in port now for almost a week waiting for me, the pair had evidently been soothed by the warm weather, and the trials of their previous months' hardship were fading in memory. However, their tranquility was quickly being eroded by the anxious expectation of 4500 kilometers of sailing a twelve-metre plastic sieve across the mid-Atlantic to Brazil via Cape Verde.

And yours truly was the only other crew member to help them out. Yes, that's a crew member with limited sailing experience, to say the least.

Now, most sensible novice sailors might attempt their first Atlantic crossing by taking part in the ARC, the Atlantic Rally for Cruisers. This is an annual event whereby you can join a flotilla of boats with similarly enthusiastic amateurs, but able and generally well-heeled sailors crossing the Atlantic to the Caribbean en mass in the best window weather (November/December), backed up by the safety of support and communications befitting a large scale venture to ensure a safe passage.

Most people who do this probably plan ahead for at least a year.

However, that's boring. Me, Hendrick and Ginny were not doing this. We were relative nautical novices, sailing a clapped out fifth-hand plastic bucket full of holes southwards across four thousand kilometres of bad-ass Atlantic, crossing the equator to northern Brazil. On our own. The principal safety aid was a second-hand satellite phone. Period.

Now, this was a risky business to say the least, and when I look back, I must have been mad. Or Greece must have been really bad. It is said that you have a far better chance of survival on the slopes of Everest, than you do lost overboard at sea. I concur one hundred per cent, not that I've climbed Everest. Yet.

When you are in a small boat in potentially lethal conditions, you have to have total confidence in your Captain, your fellow crew members, their ability, your own ability, your vessel's ability, and a deep knowledge of, and respect for Mother Nature. Of the points made in this preceding sentence, the only certainties were that the boat was small, and Mother Nature did indeed hold my respect!

For those of you who have never sailed, if you see a boat in a Marina, even a relatively modest one, it seems quite big. However, take that boat and sail it out past the breakwater to the middle of thousands of square miles of empty ocean and the boat becomes very, very, very small very bloody quickly. Stay on it without the means to get off for days on end and it gets even smaller.

If there's a problem, it's not like you just say "Bugger this, I've had enough of this, I'm off, I'll see you later." You are there for the duration. I now reckon Hendrick's natural "Sarth Ifreekun" macho demeanour had changed the name of the boat from Small bird to Big Bird. Big it most definitely wasn't.

All told, we spent about a week in Gran Canaria getting supplies, making repairs, stowing all sorts of spares, checking the emergency kit, whilst all the time keeping an eye on the weather forecast. We would be taking a week's hop down to Cape Verde prior to the long leg to Salvador in North East Brazil.

Along with a gib and mainsail, the boat had an inboard Perkins diesel engine, known in the marine world as one of the most reliable in the world.   However, these engines, with age, do tend to leak a lot of oil, and Big Bird's was no exception.

Due to this and Ginny's insistence, because of the environmental catastrophe that a couple of drops of oil in the Ocean might cause, Hendrick decided to strip the whole thing down prior to departure to try and remedy the problem.

I had told him it probably would be better to let sleeping dogs leak, as here we were a day or two away from setting forth across the Atlantic and we didn't want any un-expected surprises, and wouldn't it be nicer to soak up the sun in the waterfront bars?

Wasn't to be had. Any kind of money-spending was off the table as it had become very apparent in the first few days that Hendrick and Ginny were on a shoestring budget. To put it nicely.

Nope, Hendrick was set in his mind, so I stripped down to my shorts and helped him for the next eight hours in 40 degrees of heat in the cramped engine bay stripping the bloody Perkins.

Each of us being probably three kilos lighter, by torch and battery light we eventually got the damn thing back together. A press on the starter, a few puffs and grunts, and the good old Perkins spluttered into life, to our enormous relief. The oil which still dripped out of the seals wasn't however, and it was plain to see that the leak was much worse than before. Still, that was that. We'd have to live with it.

I'll take this moment to point out that your's truly, who'd offered to crew for free for the adventure, was doing all this maintenance effort free of charge. If this wasn't enough, I was also being politely requested by Hendrick to contribute to the mooring fees, fuel and food as well as having paid my flights there and back from Brazil. The only thing I was getting out of this was the dreamy experience of a "free" crossing of the Atlantic under sail. As it was, it turned out to be three weeks of hell.

So, Perkins back to life, stores aboard, Big Bird bursting at the seams (literally) with pre-packed non-perishables, cans, water, you name it, the day for departure came. The weather was good, so we enthusiastically set sail from Grand Canaria on a heading of 190 degrees for the week's sail to Cape Verde. Warm wind, blue ocean, sun glaring down, spirits were good.

The First Leg – Gran Canaria to Cape Verde

It was a good preamble. The weather remained wonderful, the seas were reasonably calm, a helpful north-easterly wind pushed us along nicely and frequent visits by pods of dolphins provided delightful entertainment. The sailing went well enough, allowing the three of us to get to know each other's "ways" in this compact environment. And here was the first major problem. How does it go? "Two's company…….."

It was Ginny. Well, it was actually me and Ginny. I hadn't known until it was too late, but she was a staunch vegetarian. No meat or fish of any kind. And, as is nearly always the case with these people of extreme beliefs, they tend to be very opinionated, self-righteous and downright inflexible.

In Ginny's case, to kill any animal - or fish - was a crime. So, no meat or fish was allowed on the boat. I remember bringing a can of frankfurters on board once before setting off for Cape Verde and it was hugely frowned upon. I huddled in the cockpit with my own pan and plate like a leper.

Now, just think about this for a moment. You're about to spend three weeks floating over an enormous fresh fish tank, with nothing to do but, well, fish! But sorry..... no fishing!

Not only that, due to space and safety, the amount of beer on board was minimum, just enough to allow for an occasional celebratory tinny at sundown, so the boat was pretty much dry. Dry in an alcoholic sense as it certainly wasn't in the oceanic sense. Just about every seal leaked.

Unfortunately, the unreliability of the Perkins was brought to light on that first leg – it was a bloody nightmare. It wouldn't run for more than an hour before having to be switched off, side panels removed and topped up with oil. And here's the worst part. The leaking oil discharged into the bilges, where it mixed with sea water.

Now, although I consider myself a man who looks after the environment, the leaking oil was of such minute quantities even I agreed that it could be pumped out into the sea with the bilge pump without damage to marine life. However, environmentalist-veggie Commie-bitch Ginny wouldn't have it, meaning we – that's Hendrick and yours truly - were obliged to spend hours in burning temperatures in the bilges in a boat that's pitching and rolling all over the place, using an oversized syringe to suck up the dirty water into empty plastic bottles, to be stored until we got to the next port. Even Hendrick thought she was bloody mad, but evidently his Captain's authority excluded his missus.

Apart from that, we made Cape Verde without too much drama.

Ever been to Cape Verde? It's weird. Africa meets Europe in the middle of the Ocean. It's now becoming more and more tourist exploited and has always been an important staging post for blue-water sailors. It's here that I learned something else about sailing. There are two types of sailors. Those who have money, and those who don't. And yes, you know which camp I was in.

We's just spent seven days at sea. Seven days of no hot water, limited sleep, and dried egg and lentils. I was desperate for a hot shower and a steak, washed down with red wine and cold beer. However, the marina fees were twenty-five euros a night, which was apparently way off Big Birds budget, so we stayed on anchor. And yes, ate more dried egg and lentils.

The next morning however, the need for diesel and water meant that were obliged to momentarily moor alongside the jetty, so I took advantage to get my hot shower.

We spent three more days stocking up, doing a bit of sightseeing, and preparing for the "big push" - a month on a heading of 220 degrees, destination Salvador in Brazil.

The Crossing – Three Weeks of Hell

It was a very windy evening when Hendrick announced that it was time to go. Why he picked an evening to leave and not a morning I'll never know, but he did, so we weighed anchor, hoisted the mainsail in what was probably a force six and shot away from the peace and security of Cape Verde towards an endless horizon and over four thousand kilometres of empty black ocean.

If you've ever been on a roller coaster when you shudder to the top of the first big drop, then suddenly tip over down the other side…? Well, that was the feeling! Oh shit!

I could write an entire book about the crossing. The heartaches, the arguments, the camaraderie, the near disasters, but that's for another day. I will however mention two events that stand out, simply for their brilliance.

The first happened on a sunny day, about a week into the crossing. The swell was with us, enormous slow rollers coming up behind the boat, lifting her up, and causing a gentle acceleration as Big Bird contentedly surfed down the face for a few moments before the wave left us and went on ahead.

Suddenly, and without any warning, a pod of some fifty pilot whales came up behind us and swam and dived along with us. They kept us company for a good twenty minutes until their curiosity had been satisfied and they peeled away to one side. A truly breathtaking and magnificent display by good Old Mum - she never fails.

The second was at night. I was on watch, Hendrick and Ginny asleep down below. It was a brilliant moon, a gentle breeze allowing Big Bird to make four knots. The sea was calm, and all I could hear was the hiss and bubbling of the water passing along the hull. The sky was black-blue, and I could see a million stars with a brightness you can only see away from the light-pollution of cities. The sense of complete and utter calm was magic. Total serenity.

For some reason, I suddenly felt the urge to turn around and look backwards. Don't know why, but I did. Behind us, I could see the wake of the boat lit up as if by thousands upon thousands of micro lights. Like a million stars in the water. Apparently, this phosphorescence is called bioluminescence and is caused by micro algae which emit light when disturbed.

Then, some hundred yards back, the water erupted in an explosion of light as a creature, maybe a dolphin, a whale or large fish, emerged from the depths in an eruption of silver light and crashed back into the sea. The sea very quickly composed itself back to it's blue-black sheen as if nothing had ever happened. It was a sight that will live with me for ever.

Salvador and Landfall

The days at sea wore on and on. Endless. As said, I won't go into the details of the crossing, save to mention there were quite a few good moments, quite a few bad ones, some pretty scary occurrences but fortunately we were spared any serious storms.

I actually don't think Big Bird and its crew would have survived a real Atlantic tempest. It was clear though, that as the days went by, my relationship with Ginny was souring significantly. I put it down to her total intransigence on the fishing prohibition.

As it was, it took us twenty-four days to sail from Cape Verde to Salvador. Imagine over three weeks stuck in a plastic tub with two other people being constantly tossed around, and virtually none of the basic comforts of home? As we approached the Brazilian coast, things were pretty tense on board. None of us could wait to get off.

With only a few hours left to end the nightmare, we should have been in good spirits, but we weren't. And boy, did we get our arrival wrong!

Instead of making landfall at the nearest point to Cape Verde, which would have been Natal, we had gone another thousand kilometres further south down the Brazilian coast heading for Salvador, a large port city in the state of Bahia. Now, why didn't we stop in Natal you might ask, which would have taken 10 days off the "at sea" time? I have my own thoughts on this which I'll reveal at the end of the story.

So, there we were, approaching the port of Salvador, an enormous container port with massive merchant ships all over the place, all coming in and going out. It was the early hours of the morning, still dark, blowing a bloody gale and there was a serious choppy swell.

All three of us by now were well and truly knackered, and due to the conditions, we were now having to work a two-on, one-off watch.   Such was my exhaustion that when I went below for a break, I didn't even bother getting out of my oils, as everything underneath was soaked anyway. The bed, the floor, the walls, everything dripped water.   I'd just lie there on my wet bunk, the deafening sound of Dot hammering away in the stern of the boat. (Did I mention I'd nicknamed the Perkins Dot, as in Dorothy?) Anyway, soaked and cold, Dot and the thumping of the waves smashing against the hull had no trouble in keeping me awake.

As we got closer to Salvador, the squalls had become so fierce that we'd dropped the mainsail leaving only the foresail and Dot to battle it out for us. It was pitch black, the boat was being tossed this way and that and we were barely going forward. This was a dire situation, made worse by the fact that were almost collapsing from exhaustion.

Suddenly, a violent gust tore the foresail into shreds, but neither I nor Hendrick had the energy or the will to pull it in, leaving it flapping in the wind. Now we were completely in the hands of Dot, knowing she could give up at any moment. If she did, we would be in serious trouble.

Fortunately, I think Dot was as eager to make landfall as we were, and she valiantly kept going until we made the relative calm of the outer estuary. I remember at this point, something quite surreal. Above us, in the very heavy cloud base, something was flashing, illuminating the entire sky. Lightning, I thought? It turned out to be a search and rescue plane, trying to contact us to ensure that we were OK. Apparently, we'd been spotted by some passing ship in the night who must have seen us. However, as we didn't have the radio on, we didn't realize what was going on.

I had always imagined that Salvador would be a small fishing village, nestling on a quaint little estuary, and I couldn't wait to arrive, moor up and sleep for a week. It turns out that it's one of the largest cities in Brazil and the estuary is miles wide. It's also a major oil producing region, and the river is a holding zone for dozens of old, shitty supertankers, rigs, and a multitude of support vessels.

As we came around the cardinal, things were desperate. Dot was nearly out of diesel, but Hendrick didn't dare try to fill her up, as any water in the fuel would cause her to cut out, and it was lashing down. Hendrick himself was close to passing out through sheer exhaustion, and to cap it all, we had absolutely no idea where we were going.

The city was on our starboard, rising up from the water's edge like Manhattan. We knew there was a marina there, but Hendrick had concluded it would be cheaper upriver so on we chugged. We spent the next three hours trying to locate a mooring, at the same time dodging both stationary and moving vessels. Hendrick suddenly told me to take over, staggered down the hatch and passed out.

I watched him go below, fully conscious of the fact that the only reason why I was prepared to be the last one standing was to get off this goddamned boat as fast as possible. For good.

The sun was now beginning to come up, and I decided to motor very slowly back out towards the marina. As I approached it, I realized that I had to put out the fenders alone as Hendrick and Veggie were unconscious below.

I set the tiller and skidded across the soaking deck a bit too enthusiastically, slipped and a sharp cleat slamming into the side of my knee was the only thing that stopped me going over the side. I didn't actually faint but God Almighty, it hurt. I couldn't move my leg, convinced I had smashed the kneecap and hung on to one of the shrouds trying to stay on board.

My scream of agony had been loud enough to jerk Hendrick back to consciousness, as his head suddenly appeared from below and he came to help.

It was now eight in the morning, it was pissing down, we were exhausted, we were soaked and hungry, and we certainly weren't friends anymore. We had managed to tie up against a wooden jetty and you could almost hear Big Bird and Dot panting. We had sailed across almost five thousand kilometers of ocean in a plastic bucket and survived!

Resisting the desire to collapse, and without a word to Hendrick or Veggie who by now had also surfaced, I managed to crawl below, grab my passport and limped off the boat on one leg, carrying a can of twelve per cent beer that I'd been keeping for that very moment. I had to fight off the tears, it was that emotional.

Parting Company

Maybe I shouldn't say this in case any Baiano reads this, but Salvador is a shithole. A mass of humanity, hardly any of them with a pot to piss in. Well at least that's what I saw. Perhaps there are some nice bits, but if there are, they aren't near the port.

We spent a few days getting the paperwork sorted out, cleaning out the boat, and me getting my gear together as I'd most definitely decided to jump ship, catch a flight down to Rio. The plan was to spend a week recovering with an old contact who was working there.

Hendrick and Veggie, sorry Ginny (relations had thawed somewhat) were going to coast-hop down and meet me there. That was the agreement as we parted company on the jetty, and I walked up away with my kitbag. As it was, I never saw them again.

As most of my clothes were still sodden, I gave them to a dark-skinned fellow who worked at the marina. He seemed very grateful. I jumped in a taxi and headed to the Ibis Hotel at the airport ready for a morning flight south.

Once I'd checked in, I found room forty-seven, and just stood in the doorway not knowing what to think. A warm, dry double-bed that wasn't either moving or reeking of diesel fuel. A shower, hot and powerful, and I could go to the bog and wipe my bum with dry toilet paper - paradise! Then a strange urge came over me, probably a sense similar to that of having survived a near death experience. I went over to the phone and called my ex-girlfriend Chantal in France. Who's Chantal? Well, that's another story.

Cleaned and rested, surprisingly for only a few hours, I went down to the bar to write my diary over a few cold beers and a steak. My emotions were very mixed. I felt both elated, an enormous sense of achievement but at the same time completely exhausted. The experience had drained me like nothing I'd ever experienced before. I also felt extremely alone.

The following morning, I flew down to Rio back to the civilized world.

Footnote

As I mentioned, Hendrick and Ginny never made contact again. The initial agreement had been that I would accompany them across the Atlantic and then we would see how things go from there. However, there was no doubt in my mind that they would not be able to go from Brazil to South Africa just the two of them. Even three was pushing it.

I also made some enquires and all the marinas in and around Rio would be completely off Big Bird's budget.

I emailed them from Rio, and all they said was that they'd be taking their time getting down to Rio where they would spend a few days restocking, and then would head on across the southern Atlantic to Cape Town.

And that's all I know. I also suspect that the reason we didn't stop in Natal and pushed on a further thousand kilometres south down the coast of Brazil was that they either suspected I would leave as soon as we hit land, or they had made up their mind they didn't want me to continue.

After all the hazards we'd faced together, all I can say is that I must have been a shitty deckhand.

Oh, I do admit to capsizing the rubber dinghy once.

PART III - JACKS' LOG

Hopefully, by the time you read this chapter, you'll have read most, if not all of the stories, and, hopefully again, enjoyed them.

As said, all true, names changed for obvious reasons and a little literary license here and there to liven things up.

Many of the places and names I recommend you look up on Google and you'll see images of some of the awesome places I've been.

If you have a look on my Instagram Page @jackballentynebooks or my Website www.jackballentyne.co.uk you'll see some of them posted there.

The majority of those places can still be visited, although the majority much more restrictive and organized than older times.

One of the biggest challenges in writing this book was to decide which stories to include and which to omit. I have many, many more anecdotes. For example, my years in the Motor Exhibitions industry, although little to do with travel, provided some outrageous, dangerous and hysterical tales. Looking behind the scenes of this industry makes Top Gear look like Blue Peter. Maybe I'll get around to writing about that one day, but that would necessitate a book unto itself.

Except for the lead up to the Atlantic crossing, I didn't include the story about driving alone in a beat-up old Jeep from the UK to Greece via the Balkans, with a view to living on a Greek Island. What happened in those bizarre six months, not only in Greece but Albania was a real eye opener to the enormous social and cultural differences that still exist in Europe. Some things I saw and experienced, especially towards the animal kingdom, would turn your stomach. Another complete book.

Or, driving an open-top (in fact no top at all) hand-built sports car from Buenos Aires to Southern Patagonia, a six thousand kilometer round trip. From one hundred degrees baking sunshine to minus ten degrees and snow, hail stones the size of golf balls, corrupt police officers, it was an incredible journey. This was ten years before Jeremy Clarkson did a similar escapade with the BBC, getting into all sorts of hot water. We did it on our own, no back up, just a few blokes, no GPS, a few paper maps, a box of Cuban Cigars and a good stock of Malbec wine. Awesome scenery, awesome people, and an awesome experience. Again, another book.

Then there's the six years spent in France trying to become a Frenchman.

I've not mentioned my two round-the-world trips, or the extended visits to Jamaica, America, The Scottish tours, Cyprus, Crete, Namibia, Fiji, Finland, Sweden, Italy …. Hell, I could go on.

I'm now into my 50's and having led this – how can I say? - "colourful" life, has had its consequences. Married once, nearly married again, no kids and no ties. This all means no roots. I was finally ready to settle down with my sole mate a few years back (remember I mentioned Chantal?) but due to circumstances beyond my control, it never happened, and I moved on.

Like I said at the beginning, you only have one chance at life, and in my humble opinion, the wonder of travel and adventure can only improve you both spiritually and mentally. I've had a bloody good go. "Get in there kid, before it's too late" as Rod Stewart sang.

Whilst we try to convince ourselves that the world is getting better, in my opinion it is only improving for a very few. Yes, it is *changing* for pretty much the entire global population, but getting better? The world is, in many ways, deteriorating socially and environmentally thanks to modern mankind and his hunger for money and the limitless divulgence of information.

I feel sorry for those young people who may want to experience our planet as I have, but which is today more complex, travel is more commercial, more restricted and in many places a lot more dangerous.

Although I've spent most of my life in a bit of a haze, I've never done anything bad. I've never won anything, never had to borrow or beg for money, or inherited it, I've gotten by on my own. When we surfed, skied and drank, we never caused trouble, never threw litter, never damaged anything, or sprayed graffiti. I consider myself ever respectful to anyone, no matter their standing. Disrespect simply isn't in my nature. Sure, I got into the occasional rumpus, but no bad stuff.

I believe in hard work, loyalty, courtesy, respect, honour and truth, and, as you know, I am rugby man. I am not a racist, but I am a nationalist. That each nation has its own identity, customs and language I believe makes our planet that much better. I am very worried by globalization as it is, in my mind, driven solely by commercial consideration and eroding values and customs.

I am an Englishman through and through, I will always consider this fair isle to be home, and when the sun shines, the English countryside can be stunning. However, each time I return to the UK, I become more and more upset and vow to leave again.

Traditions disappearing, or worse still being banned. The green belt being eaten away for houses that shouldn't be built. Globalization is mixing races and cultures that don't always mix well, causing unrest, and then there's never ending need to make money, all the rich and famous being waved consistently in the face of everyone. I won't even mention my opinions on social media.

As I write these final words in Wiltshire, it's mid-winter, the Brexit debate – or should I say debacle – is supposedly to be put to bed with the UK cutting loose in December 2020. Meanwhile, such trivia as Strictly Come Dancing makes the front pages of supposedly serious newspapers. That's how bad things have become!

The quality of fare on TV is absolutely numbing and I can't watch England matches without having to pay. It's cold and grey outside, I can't drive to the pub as I can't have a drink, I've just got an exorbitant council tax bill and my glass is empty. Yes, time to go again.

Let's see. There's the Trans Siberian Railway, or maybe take the North-West Passage across northern Canada? Then again, I could always drive a motorbike from Canada down to Punta Arenas, and return to

Bariloche in the Argentine lake region, this time driving south down the pacific coast of Chile via O'Higgins, back down to Punta Arenas. Maybe pop over to Antarctica whilst I'm there? Or perhaps the Fish River Canyon in Namibia? Some interesting options.

Originally, this book was going to be entitled 'Memoirs of a mere mortal' which I am. But, having written it, the title changed to reflect how I've lived and how, no doubt I will continue to before heading on to be a squid.

I hope my tales have given you the desire to see more of the world and cast aside those all-inclusive packages, worry less about the treadmill and realize you only have one shot. And you do need to laugh!

So, we come to the end. Thanks for getting this far, and, as Dave Allen would have said, " Thank you, and may your God go with you".

AND THAT'S IT........FOR NOW

Printed in Great Britain
by Amazon